# 500

## mexican dishes

# 500

# mexican dishes

h Fertig

PLE

A Quintet Book

First published in the UK in 2010 by
Apple Press
7 Greenland Street
London NW1 0ND
United Kingdom

www.apple-press.com

ISBN: 978-1-84543-351-2
QTT.THME

This book was conceived, designed, and produced by
Quintet Publishing Limited
6 Blundell Street
London N7 9BH
United Kingdom

Project Editor: Asha Savjani
Series Editor: Robert Davies
Food Stylist: Fergal Connolly
Photographer: Ian Garlick
Designer: Gavin Edwards
Editorial Assistants: Camilla Barton, Tanya Laughton
Art Director: Michael Charles
Managing Editor: Donna Gregory
Publisher: James Tavendale

10 9 8 7 6 5 4 3 2 1

Printed in China by 1010 Printing International Ltd.

Shutterstock images appear on pages 13; 168; 227; 253; 277.
Stock Food images appear on pages 73 Andrew Scrivani; 103, 114 Susie M. Eising; 115 Mary Ellen Bartley; 133
Foodcollection; 167 Michael Brauner; 194 Foodcollection; 195 Food Image Source/John Kelly; 218 Andre Baranowski;
223 Valerie Janssen; 226 Ellen Silverman; 250 Bernhard Winkelmann; 276 Allison Dinner; 281 Anita Oberhauser.
Alamy images appear on page 224 © Tim Hill/Alamy.

Quintet Publishing Limited wishes to thank The Mariposa Collection, Casa Mexico (www.casamexico.co.uk)

# contents

# introduction

The Conquest of Mexico in 1521 gave rise to one of the richest culinary revolutions in history. When the Spanish explorer Hernando Cortez and his conquistadors came to the Americas in search of gold, they found instead a wealth of New World foods: chocolate, peanuts, vanilla, beans, squash, chillies, avocados, coconuts, guavas, pineapple, prickly pear cactus, sweetcorn and tomatoes.

The ancient Maya (800 BC to AD 800), whose homeland stretched from the Yucatán Peninsula on the Caribbean coast westwards to the Pacific in southern Mexico, had cultivated the "Three Sisters" of sweetcorn, beans and squash. The Aztecs, who ruled central Mexico from the 1300s until the Conquest, added chocolate, vanilla, coffee, pulque (later transformed into tequila) and chillies. In turn the Spanish brought pork, beef, lamb, citrus fruits, garlic, cheese, milk, wheat, vinegar and wine. Although the conquistadors systematically destroyed the Aztec empire and replaced it with Spanish ways, they never succeeded in extinguishing the native culture and traditions.

Food, as always, is the conduit from the past to the present. Mexican cooking today starts with ingredients that ancient peoples would have grown or gathered, raised or hunted. Ancient recipes, such as banana-leaf wrapped meats and fish, pozole, pulque, chocolate drinks and corn tortillas, are still made in Mexican kitchens. Add to that the European influences from Spanish and French colonials, and you have a vibrant culinary tradition. From the simplest family meal to a high-style dinner, Mexican food still means a fiesta of flavours, textures and colours.

# regional cuisines

A land of great geographical contrasts, Mexico ranges from desert and prairie to lush valleys, coastal lowlands, rugged sierras and tropical rainforests.

### baja
This long peninsula just south of California is famous for its fish tacos and seafood dishes.

### chihuahua
The plains of northern Mexico produce wheat, cattle and dairy products, such as the crumbly white Chihuahua cheese. Tex-Mex dishes heavy on meat and beans are popular here.

### durango
The "Wild West" of Mexico is a mountainous region in the north-central part of the country, known for its pine forests, wild game dishes and queso asadero (a melting-type cheese).

### jalisco
Blue agave reigns in this dry region of western Mexico, where the best tequila is made.

### oaxaca
Coffee is grown in this southern region and is usually prepared a la olla – laced with sugar and cinnamon and left to simmer in a large pot for hours.

### puebla
Just two hours south of Mexico City, Puebla is where the first mole sauce was prepared. Today, every household has its own special version.

### sonora

This northwestern region is famous for its wheat flour tortillas, guava cooked down into a fruit paste, prickly pear and nopal, and tamales.

### veracruz

In seaside Veracruz, fish is the most popular dish. Any fish dish a la Veracruzana means it is topped with a sauce of tomatoes, olives, capers and chillies.

### yucatán

The ancient land of the Maya on the Caribbean coast features foods marinated in achiote (a red annatto paste), then wrapped in banana leaves and cooked outdoors.

# ingredients

In Mexico, with its warm climate and long growing season, the cooking relies on fresh, local ingredients, usually grown in small plots by the householder or purchased at the mercado (market). Fresh ingredients round out the staples of the ancient cuisine built upon sweetcorn and beans, which are often used dried. With larger families, there is always someone in the kitchen to make a salsa, corn tortillas, a salad or a sweet treat.

Flavourings such as herbs and chillies help the taste of a dish, but they also add practical nutrients. Herbs such as epazote not only add flavour but also help counter the digestive effects of beans. Chillies contribute a fiery note to bland foods as well as necessary vitamin C. Meat, fish and chicken are preferably local and used sparingly; that's why you'll find fajitas or strips of grilled meat served with tortillas and condiments rather than a big steak.

Happily, many supermarkets and grocery stores outside of Mexico now include an expanded section of Hispanic products, where you can find evaporated goat's milk for cajeta, prepared dulce de leche, Mexican chocolate, dried epazote, tinned chillies, salsas, dried beans and much more. In the fresh produce aisle, fresh chillies, avocados and coriander are as easy to find as peas, beans and parsley, while tortillas have become so common that children today have no concept of their country of origin.

### beans
Used both fresh and dried. The most common Mexican beans are black beans and pintos. Small beans are often served refrito (refried in lard) or de la olla (simmered in broth).

### cactus

A spiky desert plant used as a fruit, vegetable and base for making tequila. Nopales or cactus pads are boiled, then used in salads and side dishes. Prickly pear fruits are made into jams, jellies and syrups. Blue agave pinas or fruits go into the production of tequila.

### cheese & dairy

These are used mainly for finishing a dish. Queso fresco is a crumbly, white cow's milk cheese; aged queso fresco is called anejo. Queso blanco or Monterey Jack cheese is mild and meltable. Chihuahua is similar to mild cheddar. Queso quesadilla and asadero, mozzarella-like cheeses, are used as a filling for quesadillas. Cotija is an aged, hard grating cheese similar to Parmesan and mainly used to garnish vegetable dishes. Crèma is Mexican-style crème fraîche, a blend of sour cream and cream.

### chillies

Used both fresh and dried to add flavour, colour and contrast to bland foods. Even if used fresh, many chillies like poblanos are roasted before using in a recipe (see page 14). Fresh chillies include: Anaheim, guajillo, habañero, jalapeño, New Mexico, poblano and serrano. Dried chillies include ancho, cascabel, chilli negro and chipotle. Dried chillies are usually soaked in water to soften before using or are ground into a powder as a seasoning. Chillies offer a variety of heat, from the milder Hatch, New Mexico and jalapeño to the medium-heat poblano/ancho to the hotter-than-hot habañero. Start with jalapeño and move up the chilli chain to reach your level of hotness.

### herbs

Fresh or dried epazote, similar to oregano, and fresh coriander are used in many dishes. Epazote helps counter the digestive effects of beans and other ingredients, while coriander adds a fresh, herby note and green garnish that rounds out the flavour of cheese and chillies.

### fruits

Mango, papaya, coconut and pineapple – always plentiful in Mexico because of its warm climate – are eaten fresh as well as in sauces and desserts.

### lemons & limes

Key limes, small indigenous fruits, are more sour than the more common, larger Persian limes. Lemons came in with the Spanish. Both fruits thrived in Mexico's mild climate, where their refreshing qualities are welcome in the heat.

### piloncillo

Brown, semi-unrefined sugar, formed into a cone and used to sweeten desserts, coffee and fruit dishes.

### seeds

Pepitas or roasted pumpkin seeds and piñons or pine nuts are used in sauces and as a garnish.

### sweetcorn

Used fresh and dried. Corn masa is a flour made from sweetcorn kernels soaked in lime and dried (pozole), then ground into flour for corn tortillas and tamales. Instant corn masa flour is the variety most available from specialist Mexican food stores and is easiest to use. Dried corn husks are used to enclose tamales before steaming.

### tomatoes

Both tinned and fresh tomatoes are the essential ingredient for fresh and cooked salsas. Small, tart tomatillos are green tomatoes encased in a stiff husk, often used for a green salsa served with chicken and fish.

# equipment

Mexican food can be made with the usual indoor kitchen equipment: blender or food processor, chopping board and knives, measuring cups and spoons, pots and pans, garlic press, grater and wooden spoons. Outdoors, a simple barbecue with a lid and barbecue equipment such as grill tongs and spatula are enough to get you started. But if you want to take a very authentic approach to Mexican cuisine, you might want to check out the following:

### cazuela
This glazed earthenware pot is used to cook moles, beans, sweetcorn and stews.

### comal
This cast-iron griddle pan is used to warm tortillas and to make carne asada. You can also use a cast-iron frying pan or a ridged grill pan.

### metate y mano
With a slightly concave base made of lava rock and a heavy cylinder held in your hand, you grind corn, spices, cacao beans or other hard ingredients.

### molcajete
This pestle and mortar, usually made of stone, is the traditional way to make guacamole. It's also good for mashing garlic or making fresh salsas.

### molinillo
This wooden whisk, held between your two palms, is the traditional way to add froth to chocolate beverages.

### tortillero
The tortilla press is a hinged metal gadget. You place a ball of corn tortilla dough on the bottom, then use the lever to press the top down and create a flat tortilla.

### vitrolero
Used for aguas frescas, this large glass container with a spout, common in Mexican markets, is also great for lemonade and other cold drinks.

# basic recipes

A typical Mexican meal depends on freshly made basic foods – a homemade corn or flour tortilla, a fresh pico de gallo, cactus "nopalitos" made tender and delicious or crisp fried tortilla chips. The better these basics, the better the overall flavour in the meal. Salsas, or "sauces" in Mexican cuisine, can be made from raw ingredients – cruda – or cooked. However they're made, salsas add a wealth of colour, texture and flavour to even the most simple dish. The blend of fresh herbs and spices makes each different salsa dish unique.

## roasted chillies

Chillies are used, both fresh and dried, in many dishes. But even when used fresh, many chillies are roasted before using in a recipe. To roast a fresh chilli, hold it with a long-handled fork over a gas flame, place it on a baking sheet under the grill, or put it on a barbecue. Turn the chilli until it is blackened and blistered all over. Place the roasted chilli in a sealable plastic bag, close the bag and let it steam for 5 minutes. Remove the skin under cold, running water. Then remove the stems and seeds and chop the chilli.

Be careful when handling fresh chillies. The seeds and membranes contain 80 per cent of the chilli's heat-producing capsaicin, so wear food-handler's gloves as you work with them or wash your hands thoroughly after chopping and removing the seeds and membranes.

# pico de gallo

This "rooster's beak" fresh garnish is a must-have with tacos, burritos and even slow-simmered dishes. It got its name from the tradition of picking up the raw garnish with thumb and forefinger, a shape that resembles a rooster beak pecking the ground.

3 plum tomatoes, chopped
½ small red onion, chopped
60 ml (¼ cup) fresh lime juice

2 tbsp chopped fresh coriander
2 tbsp chopped fresh jalapeño pepper
1½ tsp salt

Stir all ingredients together. Serve at room temperature. Makes about 360ml (12 fl. oz).

# soft corn tortillas

The Aztecs called their flat griddle cakes made with ground hominy flour tlaxcalli. The Spanish conquistadors renamed them "tortillas" after the round cake they knew in Spain. Whatever you call them, freshly made corn tortillas are delicious. Use a tortilla press to make these traditional accompaniments to any Mexican meal.

260 g (9 oz) corn masa flour
¼ tsp salt

300 ml (10 fl. oz) warm water, or more if necessary

Place the flour and salt in a bowl. Stir in the water to make a soft dough, adding a little more water if necessary. Divide the dough into 16 portions and form each portion into a ball. Cover with a damp cloth to keep the dough moist. Place each ball between two unopened sandwich bags, then press to a 12.5- to 15-cm (5- to 6-in) round in a tortilla press. Preheat an ungreased frying pan over medium-high heat. Cook each tortilla for 1 minute on each side or until golden in spots. Cover with a damp tea towel until ready to serve. Makes 16 (12.5- to 15-cm/5- to 6-inch) tortillas.

# fried tortilla chips

Freshly made soft corn tortillas are delicious to serve warm, but they're not as easy to make into fried tortilla chips as corn tortillas are, as they have more moisture than the manufactured kind. So use your favorite store-bought corn tortilla to make these chips. Serve with salsa or bake with shredded cheeses, chillies, onion and coriander for nachos.

12 (15-cm/6-in) corn tortillas                    salt
vegetable oil for frying

On a flat surface, stack 4 tortillas on top of each other, making 3 stacks of tortillas. Using a pizza wheel or a sharp knife, slice each tortilla stack into 8 triangles. In a deep fat fryer or a large, deep frying pan, heat 5 cm (2 in) of vegetable oil to 175°C (350°F/Gas mark 5). Fry the triangles in batches until golden brown and crisp, about 30-60 seconds. Remove with a slotted spoon, drain on kitchen towels and salt to taste. Serve right away or store in an airtight container at room temperature for up to 2 days. Makes 8 dozen.

# homemade flour tortillas

Spanish settlers to Mexico brought wheat flour with them, which was then made into a version of the corn tortilla. Homemade flour tortillas, hot off the griddle, taste wonderful and can be used for quesadillas, burritos and more.

300 g (10 oz) plain flour                    ³/₄ tsp salt
2 tsp baking powder                          240 ml (9 fl. oz) warm water

Place the flour, baking powder and salt in a bowl. Stir in the water to make a soft dough, adding a little more water if necessary. Divide the dough into 12 portions and form each portion into a ball. Cover with a damp cloth to keep the dough moist and leave to rest for 15 minutes. Roll out each ball of dough on a floured surface to a 23-cm (9-in) diameter round. Heat an ungreased frying pan over medium-high heat. Cook each tortilla for 1 minute per side, pressing down with a spatula for several seconds, or until browned and blistered in spots. Remove from the pan and start cooking the next tortilla. Stack the cooked tortillas on top of each other, cover with a tea towel and place in a sealable plastic bag to steam until ready to serve. Makes 12 (23-cm/9-in) tortillas.

## nopalitos

Nopales or pads of prickly pear cactus become integral parts of soups, salsas and salads when they're carefully trimmed of their prickly spines and cooked. When these pads are sliced into strips, they become nopalitos. You'll find tinned nopales at Mexican suppliers.

**450 g (1 lb) tinned nopales**
**1 fresh jalapeño or serrano pepper, stemmed and deseeded**

Holding the cactus pads with oven gloves or a towel, slice off the prickly spines and the thorny edge of the pad. If necessary, peel the cactus pad. Cut the trimmed pad into 6-mm (¼-in) wide strips. Bring a large pot of water to the boil over a high heat. Add the sliced cactus strips and the whole chilli. Cook, uncovered, until the cactus is tender when pricked with a knife, about 7-8 minutes. Drain, rinse with cold water and use right away or keep covered in the refrigerator for up to 5 days.

## basic mole

Mole, a sauce made from many different ground ingredients, comes from the word molli meaning "concoction". Legend has it that the first mole was served at a convent in the central Mexican town of Puebla de Los Angeles as a special dish for a visiting dignitary. Today, every household has its own version of mole (and you can find many different varieties at the supermarket), but all agree that mole tastes best with poultry – from the indigenous Mexican turkey known as gaujolote, to domestic turkey or chicken. Moles usually contain a variety of ground chillies, roasted nuts or seeds, green plantain and a hint of chocolate to deepen the flavour.

2 tbsp ground dried ancho chilli
170 g (6 oz) whole blanched almonds
45 g (1½ oz) diced green plantain
1 tsp ground cinnamon
1 clove garlic
2 soft corn tortillas (homemade or bought), torn
  into pieces

2 tbsp roasted pumpkin seeds
28 g (1 oz) dark chocolate
475 ml (16 fl. oz) chicken stock
80 g (3 oz) chopped tinned tomatoes, with juice
salt to taste

In a blender or food processor, grind the chilli powder, almonds, plantain, cinnamon, garlic, tortilla pieces, pumpkin seeds and chocolate with half of the chicken stock until puréed but grainy. Pour the mixture into a saucepan, add the remaining chicken stock and tomatoes, and simmer, stirring, over medium heat. Cook, stirring, until the chocolate melts and the flavours have blended, about 5 minutes. Season with salt to taste. Serve as a cooking or finishing sauce with poultry. Will keep, chilled, for up to 3 days. Makes about 475 ml (16 fl. oz).

### basic mole variations

**yellow mole**: Instead of the basic recipe, in a blender or food processor, process 15 guajillo or Amarillo chillies, roasted, stemmed, deveined and deseeded; 1 380 g (13 oz) tin tomatillos with liquid; 2 cloves minced garlic; ½ teaspoon ground cumin; ½ teaspoon dried oregano;

and ½ teaspoon ground cinnamon, until smooth. Season to taste. Bring to the boil over a medium-high heat, reduce heat and simmer for 15 minutes to let flavours blend.

**green mole**: Instead of the basic recipe, purée 2 380 g (13-oz.) tins tomatillos, 40 g (1½ oz) finely chopped onion, 40 g (1½ oz) toasted almonds, 1 tablespoon freshly chopped coriander and 3 tablespoons diced green chillies in a food processor or blender. Season to taste with salt and pepper.

**doctored mole**: Instead of the basic recipe, start with a store-bought mole. Doctor the mole with bottled smoked chipotle sauce, chopped garlic, honey and/or chopped fresh coriander, to taste.

## tomatillo salsa

Tart, tangy and pale green, tomatillo salsa is usually served with chicken, pork or fish. Tomatillos, smaller and greener cousins of the red beefsteak tomato, have papery husks that enclose the small fruits; remove the husks before using.

680 g (1½ lb) fresh tomatillos
20 g (⅔ oz) chopped fresh coriander
80 ml (3 fl. oz) fresh lime juice

salt to taste
1 jalapeño pepper, stemmed and deseeded

Remove the husks from the tomatillos and discard. Arrange the tomatillos on a baking sheet in a single layer and roast in a 230°C (450°F/Gas mark 8) oven until lightly browned (about 20 minutes). Leave to cool. In a blender or food processor, place the cooled tomatillos, coriander, jalapeño and lime juice. Process until somewhat smooth. Add salt to taste. Will keep, covered, in the refrigerator for up to 3 days. Makes about 500 ml (1 pint).

### tomatillo salsa variations

**green tomato salsa**: Prepare the basic recipe, using the same quantity of fresh, small, green tomatoes, cored, in place of tomatillos. Add sugar to taste.

**pantry shelf tomatillo salsa**: Prepare the basic recipe, using 250 g (9 oz) tinned tomatillos and 1 100-g (4-oz) tin chopped jalapeño in place of the fresh tomatillos and jalapeño. Just stir in the coriander, lime juice and salt to taste.

**grilled tomatillo salsa**: Prepare the basic recipe, but instead of roasting the tomatillos, husk them, brush with olive oil, and grill over medium-high heat, turning often, until they have good grill marks.

**poblano tomatillo salsa**: Prepare the basic recipe, using a fresh poblano in place of the jalapeño.

## pineapple salsa

Golden and tangy fresh pineapple salsa is delicious with fish and shellfish, chicken and pork dishes. Try it on grilled chicken tacos and fish tostadas, or alongside pork carnitas.

300 g (10 oz) chopped fresh pineapple
20 g ($^2/_3$ oz) chopped fresh coriander
1 fresh jalapeño pepper, stemmed and deseeded

$^1/_2$ tsp crushed red chilli flakes
salt

Place the pineapple, coriander, jalapeño pepper and chilli flakes in a blender or food processor. Process until somewhat smooth. Add salt to taste. Will keep, covered, in the refrigerator for up to 3 days. Makes about 600 ml (1$^1/_4$ pints).

### pineapple salsa variations

**pantry shelf pineapple salsa**: Prepare the basic recipe, using tinned pineapple in fruit juice, drained, in place of fresh pineapple. Add sugar to taste.

**papaya salsa**: Prepare the basic recipe, using fresh sliced papaya in place of fresh pineapple. Add a little lime juice to taste.

**mango salsa**: Prepare the basic recipe, using fresh sliced mango in place of fresh pineapple. Add a little lime juice to taste.

**strawberry & pineapple salsa**: Prepare the basic recipe, using 150 g (5 oz) hulled and sliced fresh strawberries in place of 150 g (5 oz) of the pineapple.

## salsa cruda

Made from raw, fresh ingredients, this salsa is perfect with tortilla chips and a frosty margarita or a Mexican beer.

2 cloves garlic, minced
40 g (1½ oz) finely chopped onion
75 g (2½ oz) grated fresh jicama
75 g (2½ oz) finely chopped cucumber
1 fresh jalapeño pepper, stemmed, deseeded and finely chopped

10 g (½ oz) chopped fresh coriander
450 g (1 lb) firm, ripe tomatoes, stemmed and chopped
juice of 2 limes
salt and pepper

Combine all ingredients in a bowl. Season to taste and leave to sit at room temperature until ready to serve. Makes about 500 ml (1 pint).

**salsa cruda variations**

**frozen salsa cruda**: Prepare the basic recipe. Freeze the salsa in a metal bowl, stirring every 30 minutes, until slushy, about 4 hours. Serve with chilled, cooked shrimp or half-shell oysters.

**golden salsa cruda**: Prepare the basic recipe, using yellow tomatoes in place of the red tomatoes and yellow pepper in place of jalapeño. Add ½ teaspoon ground chipotle.

**cherry tomato salsa cruda**: Prepare the basic recipe, using halved cherry tomatoes in place of the red tomatoes.

**mixed tomato salsa cruda**: Prepare the basic recipe, using an assortment of fresh tomatoes in place of the red tomatoes.

# mango & lime salsa

Tropical mangoes and the small Key limes of coastal Mexico combine to make a fresh salsa that is delicious with grilled fish and shellfish.

2 cloves garlic, minced
40 g (1½ oz) finely chopped onion
1 jalapeño pepper, stemmed, deseeded and
    finely chopped

10 g (½ oz) chopped fresh coriander
300 g (10 oz) chopped peeled mango
juice of 1 Persian lime or 2 Key limes
salt and pepper to taste

Combine all ingredients in a bowl. Season to taste and leave to sit at room temperature until ready to serve. Will keep, covered, in the refrigerator for up to 3 days. Bring to room temperature before serving.

### mango & lime salsa variations

**frozen mango & lime salsa**: Prepare the basic recipe. Freeze the salsa in a metal bowl, stirring every 30 minutes, until slushy, about 4 hours.

**papaya & lime salsa**: Prepare the basic recipe, using fresh chopped papaya in place of the mango.

**pineapple, mango & lime salsa**: Prepare the basic recipe, using 150 g (5 oz) chopped fresh pineapple in place of 150 g (5 oz) of the chopped mango.

**mango & orange salsa**: Prepare the basic recipe, adding 150 g (5 oz) chopped orange to the ingredients.

## salsa roja

Salsa roja, or red salsa from Mexico City, is a cooked version most often served with enchiladas. It's also delicious drizzled on eggs, quesadillas or steak.

6 large, ripe tomatoes
3 serrano chillies
3 tbsp chicken bouillon powder
2 tbsp olive oil

3 cloves garlic, minced
40 g (1$\frac{1}{2}$ oz) chopped onion
salt to taste

Place the tomatoes and serrano chillies in a medium saucepan with enough water to cover. Bring to the boil. Reduce the heat and simmer until the tomato skins are peeling off and the tomatoes are soft but not mushy, about 5 minutes. Remove $\frac{1}{2}$ cup of the hot cooking water and whisk it with the chicken bouillon in a small bowl until completely dissolved. Remove the tomatoes and chillies with a slotted spoon and leave to cool for a few minutes, then peel off the tomato skins and stem and seed the chillies. Place the bouillon mixture, peeled tomatoes and deseeded chillies in a blender or food processor, and pulse to process for just a few seconds until blended but still chunky. Heat the olive oil in a large sauté pan over medium-high heat, then sauté the garlic and onion until softened, about 2 minutes. Stir in the tomato mixture and cook, stirring, until the sauce has thickened (about 6–8 minutes). Season to taste and serve hot. Makes about 700 ml (1½ pints).

**salsa roja variations**

**chunky pantry shelf salsa roja**: Prepare the basic recipe, using 150 g (5 oz) tinned chopped plum tomatoes with liquid in place of the fresh tomatoes and 1 100-g (4-oz) tin jalapeño in place of serrano chillies. Mix them with the bouillon concentrate that's been dissolved in 125 ml (4 fl. oz) hot water and proceed with the recipe.

**grilled tomato salsa roja**: Prepare the basic recipe, but instead of boiling the tomatoes and serrano chillies, grill them until you have good grill marks and the skins are papery. Remove their skins, stems and seeds and finely chop. Instead of the tomato-boiling water, use 125 ml (4 fl. oz) hot water, and proceed with the recipe.

**salsa d'oro**: Prepare the basic recipe, using 6 medium yellow tomatoes in place of the 6 red tomatoes and 1 large yellow bell pepper in place of the serrano chillies. Add ½ teaspoon ground dried chipotle and proceed with the recipe.

**easy salsa roja**: Prepare the basic recipe, using 300 g (10 oz) tinned tomato purée in place of fresh tomatoes. Seed, stem and chop serrano chilli, and sauté with the onion and garlic. Add the tomato purée and salt to taste, cooking until somewhat thickened.

# pumpkin seed salsa

Made with pepitas (toasted pumpkin seeds), this salsa has a pleasant "toasty" flavour that goes well with grilled foods.

170 g (6 oz) toasted pumpkin seeds
2 cloves garlic
zest and juice of 1 lime
40 g (1½ oz) chopped fresh coriander

60 ml (2 fl. oz) olive oil
240 g (8½ oz) tinned diced tomatoes with green chillies

Place all ingredients in a blender or food processor and purée until almost smooth. Keep at room temperature until ready to serve. Makes about 500 ml (1 pint).

### pumpkin seed salsa variations

**double pumpkin seed salsa**: Prepare the basic recipe, using 120 g (4¼ oz) tinned pumpkin in place of 120 g (4¼ oz) of the tinned tomatoes with green chillies.

**doctored pumpkin seed salsa**: Instead of the basic recipe, blend 85 g (3 oz) toasted pumpkin seeds with 250 ml (½ pint) store-bought pipian (a pumpkin seed mole). Add olive oil, lime juice, tinned tomatoes with green chillies and chopped fresh coriander to taste.

**spanish almond salsa**: Prepare the basic recipe, using toasted sliced almonds in place of pumpkin seeds. Toast 170 g (6 oz) sliced almonds on a baking sheet in a 175°C (350°F/Gas mark 4) oven until lightly browned; leave to cool.

# coriander salsa

Vividly green and sharp-tasting, this salsa perks up grilled and slow-simmered foods like chicken, pork, fish and shellfish, as well as basic nachos or a plain grilled cheese.

80 g (3 oz) chopped spring onion
40 g (1½ oz) chopped fresh coriander
20 g (⅔ oz) chopped fresh Italian parsley
120 ml (4 fl. oz) vegetable oil

6 tbsp freshly squeezed lime juice
3 tbsp white wine vinegar
2 cloves garlic, minced
40 g (1½ oz) chopped jalapeño pepper

Combine all ingredients together in a bowl. Serve right away.

### coriander salsa variations

**fennel & tarragon salsa**: Prepare the basic recipe, using chopped fresh bulb fennel in place of the coriander and tarragon vinegar in place of the white wine vinegar.

**grilled onion salsa with sherry vinegar**: Prepare the basic recipe, using a grilled large red onion in place of the spring onions and sherry vinegar in place of the white wine vinegar. To grill the onion, grill slices on both sides, then chop fine.

**orange & coriander salsa**: Prepare the basic recipe, adding 150 g (5 oz) peeled sliced orange to the ingredients.

**lemon–parsley salsa**: Prepare the basic recipe, using Italian parsley in place of the coriander and lemon juice in place of lime juice.

# mango cream

Wonderful with lobster-papaya quesadillas (page 34), this multi-purpose sauce is also good on simple grilled chicken breasts or fish fillets. For extra colour and flavour, use mango salsa (page 21) as a garnish.

**2 ripe mangoes, peeled and pitted**         **fresh lemon juice to taste**
**120 ml (4 fl. oz) Mexican crèma or sour cream**

Place the mangoes, sour cream and lemon juice in a food processor or blender and purée until smooth. Use right away or cover and refrigerate for up to 2 days.

### mango cream variations

**papaya cream**: Prepare the basic recipe, using fresh papaya in place of the mango.

**sweet mango cream**: Transform this into a dessert sauce by using double cream in place of sour cream and lime juice instead of lemon juice. Add a little sugar to taste.

**mango & lime cream**: Prepare the basic recipe, using freshly grated lime zest and fresh lime juice in place of lemon juice.

**mango & orange cream**: Prepare the basic recipe, using freshly grated orange zest and fresh orange juice in place of lemon juice.

# antojitos

Antojitos ("little whims") are nibbled throughout the day. They can be called snacks or starters, but they must be delicious.

# queso al horno with tortilla chips

see variations page 43

This baked cheese starter is easy to assemble and delicious to eat.

1¹/₂ tbsp vegetable oil
1 large onion, chopped
2 fresh, large tomatoes, peeled, deseeded and
    coarsely chopped
4-6 fresh jalapeño peppers, stemmed deseeded,
    and diced

¹/₄ tsp ground dried chipotle chilli
salt to taste
900 g (2 lb) grated Monterey Jack cheese
1 small, whole jalapeño pepper, to garnish
tortilla chips, for serving

Heat the oil in a frying pan over a medium-high heat. Sauté the onion until softened, stirring occasionally, for about 10 minutes. Add the tomatoes and jalapeños and cook, stirring, until the peppers have softened, about 2 more minutes. Season to taste with ground chipotle and salt.

Preheat oven to 175°C (350°F/Gas mark 4). Place the grated cheese in a 20- to 25-cm (8- to 10-in) round baking dish at least 4 cm (1½ in) deep. Spoon the tomato mixture onto the middle of the cheese, then spread the tomato mixture to a 15-cm (6-in) diameter. Bake the cheese for 25–30 minutes or until bubbling. Garnish the centre with the whole jalapeño. Serve hot with tortilla chips.

*Serves 12*

# authentic guacamole

see variations page 44

Made with ripe, buttery avocados and tart lime juice, guacamole also has a bit of heat from chillies. For the most authentic preparation and presentation, use a molcajete – a stone pestle and mortar. When you make guacamole, you should serve it right away, as it can discolour as it sits.

2 large, ripe avocados
3 tbsp fresh lime juice
2 tbsp finely chopped fresh coriander
2 fresh jalapeño peppers, stemmed, deseeded
    and finely chopped

Halve, pit, peel and slice the avocados into a molcajete or a bowl. With the pestle of the molcajete or a fork, mash the avocados with the lime juice, coriander and jalapeño until chunky but well blended. Serve with tortilla chips or use as a garnish for other dishes.

*Makes about 375 ml (13 fl. oz)*

# market day tortas

see variations page 45

A torta in Mexico is a sandwich – usually with a meat and bean filling – on a crusty roll known as a bolillo. Street vendors often serve tortas to busy shoppers on market days, but they're just as tasty for a casual meal at home.

4 rectangular bolillos or crusty rolls, about
  15–20 cm (6-8 in) long
2 tbsp butter
340 g (³/₄ lb) chorizo sausage, casings removed
1 large onion, thinly sliced
1 (400-g/15-oz) can pinto beans, drained, or
  360 g (12 oz) frijoles refritos (page 209)

180 ml (6 fl. oz) crèma or double cream
225 g (8 oz) grated Chihuahua or Monterey Jack
  cheese
4 tbsp tomatillo salsa (page 19)

Slice the rolls lengthways and butter the cut sides. Place the rolls, cut-side down, in a large frying pan over a medium-high heat, and let brown. Remove and reserve, keeping them warm. Cook the chorizo, stirring, until well browned, about 10 minutes. Remove with a slotted spoon and reserve. Remove all but 3 tablespoons of fat from the pan, then cook the onion, stirring, until lightly browned, about 7 minutes. Stir in the beans, mashing well. Stir in the crèma and reserved chorizo and cook until bubbling.

Spoon the chorizo filling onto the bottoms of the rolls. Sprinkle each with a quarter of the cheese and 1 tablespoon of salsa and serve.

*Serves 4*

# gulf coast ceviche

see variations page 46

Originating in Peru centuries ago, ceviche travelled northwards to Mexico, where it has become part of the coastal diet. Small pieces of fish and shellfish are "cooked" with tangy lime juice to make a refreshing starter during warm months. If you like, serve ceviche in cocktail glasses or little bowls.

340 g (12 oz) fresh swordfish, tuna or mahi
    mahi cut into small cubes
125 ml (4 fl. oz) fresh lime juice
2 tbsp fresh orange juice
1 tsp ground cumin
1 tsp ground dried ancho chilli
salt and ground white pepper to taste

1 cup deseeded and finely chopped watermelon
75 g (2$^1$/$_2$ oz) freshly grated jicama (or substitute
    daikon radish sweetened with a little sugar)
80 g (3 oz) finely chopped spring onion
80 g (3 oz) finely chopped and peeled
    ripe tomato

Put the fish in a large glass or ceramic bowl. Add the lime and orange juices, cumin, ancho chilli, salt and white pepper. Mix well and cover tightly with plastic wrap. Refrigerate for 15 minutes.

Unwrap, then stir in the watermelon, jicama, spring onion and tomato. Cover tightly again and refrigerate for 15 more minutes or until the fish is turning opaque on the outside but is still rare on the inside. Serve chilled.

*Serves 8*

# lobster-papaya quesadillas with mango cream

see variations page 47

Served with a frosty margarita or a glass of chilled white wine, nothing could be finer. Papayas and mangoes from the tropical coasts of Mexico add an exotic flair to the traditional quesadilla appetizer.

100 g (4 oz) fresh goat's cheese, crumbled
1 garlic clove, crushed
40 g (1 1/2 oz) chopped onion
1/2 poblano chilli, roasted, stemmed, peeled, deseeded and diced
1/2 red pepper, roasted, peeled, deseeded and diced
2 tsp minced fresh coriander
1/4 tsp salt
2 tsp fresh lime juice
150 g (5 oz) cooked and chopped lobster meat
1 papaya, peeled, deseeded and chopped
4 (15-cm/6-in) flour tortillas (store-bought or homemade)
2 tbsp unsalted butter
mango cream (page 27), for serving

In a large bowl, combine the goat's cheese, garlic, onion, peppers, coriander, salt and lime juice. Carefully blend in the lobster and papaya. Spread some lobster mixture over half of each tortilla and fold over. Brush each tortilla with melted butter.

Heat a large non-stick frying pan over a medium-high heat. Cook the quesadillas for 3–4 minutes, turning once, until browned on both sides. Cut each into triangles and serve with mango cream.

*Serves 4*

# beef salpicon with fresh coriander & corn tortillas

see variations page 48

Salpicon, which translates as "hodge-podge", is a mixture of cold cooked meats and vegetables with a tangy dressing. It's delicious as a first course and ideal as buffet food.

1.5–1.8 kg (3$^{1}/_{2}$–4 lb) fully trimmed beef brisket
   or boneless chuck roast
1 large onion, chopped
2 bay leaves
3 cloves garlic, minced
2 cups any bottled Mexican marinade
55 g (2 oz) tinned chipotle chillies in
   adobo sauce
6 tbsp extra-virgin olive oil
60 ml (2 fl. oz) fresh lime juice

2 tbsp white wine vinegar
1 tbsp minced onion
1 clove garlic, minced
salt and pepper to taste
4 fresh, small plum tomatoes, diced
2 ripe avocados, diced
1 medium red onion, diced
170 g (6 oz) Monterey Jack cheese, cubed
20 g ($^{2}/_{3}$ oz) chopped fresh coriander, to garnish
soft corn tortillas (page 15), for serving

In a large, heavy pot, place the beef, onion, bay leaves, garlic and chipotle marinade. Add enough water to cover. Bring to the boil, then reduce the heat and simmer until the meat is tender, about 3–4 hours. Let the meat cool in the pot for 30 minutes. Remove 2 tablespoons of the liquid in the pot and reserve. Discard remaining liquid. Shred the meat and set aside. To make the dressing, place the reserved pot liquid, chipotle peppers, olive oil, lime juice, vinegar, onion, garlic, salt and pepper in a food processor. Purée until smooth. Mix the shredded meat with three-quarters of the dressing, then toss it lightly with the tomatoes, avocados, onion and cheese. Drizzle over the remaining dressing. Garnish with chopped coriander. Serve warm with hot tortillas or chilled with tortilla chips for dipping.

*Serves 12*

# fried plantains with salsa cruda

see variations page 49

Plantains are more starchy and less sweet than bananas, their botanical cousins.
In Mexico, plantains are used like potatoes. Ripe plantains are fried in place of potatoes
for a breakfast side dish, and green (unripe) plantains are transformed into these potato
crisp-like tostones. A special wooden tostonera (or the bottom of a drinking glass)
is used to flatten these partially cooked plantains.

500 ml (1 pint) vegetable oil
2 green plantains

salt and pepper to taste
salsa cruda (page 21), for serving

In a large frying pan or deep fat fryer, heat the oil to about 175°C (350°F/Gas mark 4). Peel
and slice the plantains into 2.5-cm (1-in) rounds. Place them in the hot oil and cook for
about 3 minutes while turning. Remove from oil and pat dry with a paper towel. Place each
round inside a plastic sandwich bag and flatten it with the bottom of a drinking glass or a
tostonera. Return the plantains to the hot oil for about 3 more minutes, turning, until golden
brown on both sides. Transfer to kitchen towels and pat dry. Season to taste. Serve with salsa
cruda (or with authentic guacamole, page 30, if preferred).

*Serves 4*

# chilli-spiced peanuts

see variations page 50

These spicy cacahuates or peanut snacks from Oaxaca can be addictive. They're great with a cold Mexican beer. Make a big batch and store in an airtight container to have them to hand.

15–20 small, dried, whole red chillies
4 cloves garlic, minced
3 tbsp vegetable oil

340 g (12 oz) roasted salted peanuts
1 tsp coarse salt
1 tsp ground dried ancho or chipotle chilli

In a large frying pan, combine the chillies, garlic and oil. Cook over a medium heat, stirring, for 1 minute. Add the peanuts and cook, stirring, until slightly browned and very fragrant, about 5 minutes. Remove from the heat and season with salt and ground ancho or chipotle chilli, stirring well. Leave to cool, then store in an airtight container.

*Makes 340 g (12 oz)*

# empanadas

see variations page 51

These small turnovers with their savoury picadillo filling (with a touch of sweetness) are great as starters or snacks. Use prepared pie dough for the pastry.

2 prepared pie pastry rounds
450 g (1 lb) minced beef
1 clove garlic, minced
80 g (3 oz) tinned tomato purée
80 g (3 oz) sultanas

80 g (3 oz) chopped pimiento-stuffed green
  olives
vegetable oil for frying

In a large frying pan, brown the minced beef and garlic together. Stir in the tomato purée, sultanas and olives. Set aside to cool.

Use a 7.5-cm (3-in) biscuit cutter to cut out rounds from the prepared pie dough. Spoon the filling into the centre of each round. Moisten the edges of the dough with water and fold in half, crimping the edges closed with a fork.

Heat vegetable oil in a large frying pan and fry the empanadas, turning once, until golden brown on both sides, about 2 minutes total. Transfer to kitchen towels to drain. Serve warm.

*Serves 10–12*

variations

# queso al horno with tortilla chips

see base recipe page 29

### vegetarian baked cheese with chillies
Prepare the basic recipe, using vegetarian cheese in place of Monterey Jack.

### baked cheese with chicken & chillies
Prepare the basic recipe, topping the tomato mixture with 150 g (5 oz) finely chopped cooked chicken before garnishing with the whole jalapeño.

### baked cheese with pork carnitas & chillies
Prepare the basic recipe, topping the tomato mixture with 150 g (5 oz) finely chopped pork carnitas (page 143) before garnishing with the whole jalapeño.

### baked cheese with chorizo & chillies
Prepare the basic recipe, topping the tomato mixture with 150 g (5 oz) cooked and crumbled chorizo sausage before garnishing with the whole jalapeño.

variations

# authentic guacamole

see base recipe page 30

### grilled guacamole
Halve and pit the avocados, but do not peel. Grill the avocado halves, cut-side down, outside on a medium-hot barbecue or indoors on a griddle pan for 2–3 minutes or until you have good grill marks. Proceed with the basic recipe.

### tomato guacamole
Prepare the basic recipe, adding 160 g (6 oz) chopped fresh tomato.

### fresh guacamole with lime & garlic
Prepare the basic recipe, adding 1 teaspoon minced garlic and 1 more tablespoon fresh lime juice.

### easy guacamole
Halve and pit the avocados. Scoop the flesh into a bowl, drizzle with the juice of 1 lime, mash with a fork and add salt to taste.

# market day tortas

see base recipe page 31

### grilled chicken tortas
Prepare the basic recipe, using chopped grilled chicken in place of the chorizo.

### pork carnitas tortas
Prepare the basic recipe, using pork carnitas (page 143) in place of the chorizo.

### grilled vegetable & chilli tortas
Prepare the basic recipe, using 100 g (4 oz) each sliced onion, courgette and fresh chillies, grilled, in place of the chorizo.

### taco tortas
Prepare the basic recipe, using 340 g (¾ lb) beef mince and 1 tablespoon taco seasoning in place of the chorizo. Use a red tomato salsa such as salsa cruda (page 21) in place of the tomatillo salsa.

### grilled chicken & avocado tortas
Prepare the basic recipe, using chopped grilled chicken and diced avocado in place of the chorizo and pinto beans.

variations

# gulf coast ceviche

see base recipe page 33

### fresh tuna ceviche
Prepare the basic recipe, using sashimi-grade tuna, chopped avocado in place of the watermelon and chopped fresh coriander in place of the onion.

### prawn chipotle ceviche
Prepare the basic recipe, using 8 raw, peeled and deveined medium-size prawns, cut into 1.2 cm (½-in) pieces, in place of the fish; 2 tinned chipotle chillies in adobo sauce, chopped, in place of the watermelon; and chopped fresh coriander in place of the onion.

### fresh swordfish–peach ceviche
Prepare the basic recipe, using fresh swordfish, peeled and chopped fresh peaches in place of the watermelon and chopped fresh coriander in place of the onion.

### lobster, poblano & mango ceviche
Prepare the basic recipe, using 4 fresh or frozen and thawed lobster tails – cooked in boiling water for 3 minutes or until the shells turn red, and then chopped – in place of the fish; 2 pitted and chopped mangoes in place of the watermelon; 1 poblano chilli – roasted, stemmed, deseeded and chopped – in place of the tomatoes; and chopped fresh coriander in place of the onion.

# lobster-papaya quesadillas with mango cream

see base recipe page 34

### prawn-papaya quesadillas with mango cream
Prepare the basic recipe, using 150 g (5 oz) cooked prawns in place of the lobster.

### grilled chicken-papaya quesadillas with mango cream
Prepare the basic recipe, using 150 g (5 oz) chopped grilled chicken in place of the lobster.

### grilled pork-papaya quesadillas with mango cream
Prepare the basic recipe, using 150 g (5 oz) grilled and chopped pork tenderloin in place of the lobster.

### cheese, chilli & papaya quesadillas with mango cream
Prepare the basic recipe, using 130 g (4½ oz) grated Monterey Jack cheese and 1 small deseeded and chopped jalapeño in place of the lobster.

variations

## beef salpicon with fresh coriander & corn tortillas

see base recipe page 36

### chicken salpicon with fresh coriander & corn tortillas

Prepare the basic recipe, using a 2-kg (4-lb) roasting chicken in place of brisket.

### pork salpicon with fresh coriander & corn tortillas

Prepare the basic recipe, using a 2-kg (4-lb) boneless pork rump or pork shoulder roast in place of brisket.

### lamb salpicon with fresh coriander & corn tortillas

Prepare the basic recipe, using a 2-kg (4-lb) boneless lamb shoulder roast in place of brisket.

# fried plantains with salsa cruda

see base recipe page 38

### fried plantains with tomatillo salsa
Prepare the basic recipe, using tomatillo salsa (page 19) instead of salsa cruda.

### fried plantains with pineapple salsa
Prepare the basic recipe, using pineapple salsa (page 20) instead of salsa cruda.

### fried plantains with papaya salsa
Prepare the basic recipe, using papaya salsa (page 21) instead of salsa cruda.

### fried plantains with salsa cruda, black beans & crèma
Prepare the basic recipe, adding 200 g (½ lb) tinned black beans to 250 ml
(½ pint) of the salsa cruda. Add a dollop of crèma and serve.

variations

# chilli-spiced peanuts

see base recipe page 40

### chilli-spiced mixed nuts
Prepare the basic recipe, using 340 g (12 oz) mixed nuts in place of peanuts.

### chilli-spiced pecans
Prepare the basic recipe, using 340 g (12 oz) pecan halves in place of peanuts.

### chilli-spiced almonds
Prepare the basic recipe, using 340 g (12 oz) whole blanched almonds in place of peanuts.

### chilli-piloncillo almonds
Prepare the basic recipe, using 340 g (12 oz) whole blanched almonds in place of peanuts and adding 50 g (2 oz) finely crumbled brown sugar to the seasoning at the end.

variations

# empanadas

see base recipe page 42

### turkey empanadas
Prepare the basic recipe, using turkey mince in place of the minced beef.

### crabmeat & cream cheese empanadas
Prepare the basic recipe, using 225 g (8 oz) crabmeat, 225 g (8 oz) softened cream cheese and 1 tablespoon bottled chipotle sauce in place of the minced beef, garlic, tomato purée, sultanas and olives.

### spicy chicken & cheese empanadas
Prepare the basic recipe, using 150 g (5 oz) cooked and shredded chicken, 225 g (8 oz) softened cream cheese and 1 tablespoon bottled chipotle sauce in place of the minced beef, garlic, tomato purée, sultanas and olives.

### banana-rum empanadas
Prepare the basic recipe, using 3 mashed ripe bananas and 60 ml (2 fl. oz) dark rum in place of the minced beef, garlic, tomato purée, sultanas and olives.

### sundried tomato & goat's cheese empanadas
Prepare the basic recipe, using 225 g (8 oz) softened goat's cheese, 40 g (1½ oz) chopped sundried tomatoes and 40 g (1½ oz) chopped black olives in place of the minced beef, garlic, tomato purée, sultanas and green olives.

# soups & salads

Cool and refreshing salads – some with the welcome crunch of jicama – make a hot day more bearable. When the cold nights come, hot and steamy soups with the fragrance of Mexican seasonings warm body and soul.

# desert cactus soup

see variations page 73

Thorny pads of prickly pear cactus from desert areas in northern Mexico are de-spined, cooked and then cooked with stock for this delicious soup.

80 g (3 oz) chopped onion
1 tbsp olive oil
450 g (1 lb) nopalitos (page 17), or use tinned

1 l (2 pints) chicken stock
sour cream, diced tomatoes and chopped
    coriander, to garnish

Sauté the onion in olive oil in a large saucepan over medium-high heat. Add the nopalitos and chicken stock. Bring to the boil, then reduce the heat and simmer for 15 minutes. Garnish each bowl with sour cream, diced tomatoes and coriander before serving.

*Serves 4-6*

# gazpacho with crèma & fresh coriander

see variations page 74

Brought from Spain to Mexico, this refreshing cold vegetable soup is perfect in warm weather. Top it with a dollop of Mexican crème fraîche, known as crèma, and a sprinkle of fresh coriander.

1 kg (2 lb) fresh ripe tomatoes, chopped and peeled
150 g (5 oz) peeled and finely chopped seedless cucumber
1 red pepper, deseeded and diced
1 small red onion, finely chopped
225 g ($^1/_2$ lb) country-style bread, crust removed, cut into 1.2-cm ($^1/_2$-in) pieces

60 ml (2 fl. oz) fresh lime juice
60 ml (2 fl. oz) extra-virgin olive oil
1 garlic clove, minced
$^1/_2$ tsp ground cumin
salt and pepper to taste
240 ml (8 fl. oz) crèma or sour cream, to garnish
20 g ($^2/_3$ oz) chopped fresh coriander, to garnish

Place the tomatoes in a large glass bowl. Stir in the cucumber, pepper, onion, bread, lime juice, olive oil, garlic and cumin. Season to taste with salt and pepper. Leave to stand at room temperature for 1 hour to release the vegetable juices.

Chill for at least 2 hours or up to 1 day. Serve cold in bowls, garnished with crèma, and sprinkled with coriander.

*Serves 8*

# mexican roasted sweetcorn & chilli soup

see variations page 75

Roast the corn and chilli in the oven first, then simmer them together in this tasty soup.

4 ears sweetcorn, shucked and silk removed
1 tbsp olive oil
1 large Anaheim chilli
1 tsp ground dried ancho chilli

750 ml (1½ pints) chicken stock
240 ml (8 fl. oz) double cream
salt and pepper to taste
freshly chopped coriander, to garnish

Brush the sweetcorn with olive oil. Place the sweetcorn and the Anaheim chilli on a baking sheet under the grill, turning once, until the corn kernels and chilli are blackened. Place the chilli in a plastic bag, close, and leave to steam for 5 minutes. Remove the skin under cold, running water. Stem, deseed and chop the chilli. With a paring knife, scrape the roasted kernels from each ear of sweetcorn.

Combine the chilli, sweetcorn, dried ancho and chicken broth in a saucepan over medium-high heat. Bring to the boil, then reduce the heat and leave to simmer for 5 minutes. Stir in the cream, season to taste and serve garnished with coriander.

*Serves 4–6*

# wild mushroom & chipotle soup

see variations page 76

Known as *sopa de hongos salvajes*, this dish is made during the autumn months in the sierra or mountainous areas of Oaxaca and Tlaxcala in central Mexico.

450 g (1 lb) wild mushrooms, cleaned and sliced
2 cloves garlic, minced
80 g (3 oz) chopped onion
1 tbsp olive oil

2 tinned chipotles in adobo sauce, chopped
1.5 l (3 pints) chicken stock
sour cream, diced tomatoes and chopped
   coriander, to garnish

Sauté the mushrooms, garlic and onion in olive oil in a large saucepan over medium-high heat until the mushrooms have wilted and given off their juices. Add the chipotle and chicken stock. Bring to the boil, then reduce the heat and simmer for 15 minutes. Garnish each bowl with sour cream, diced tomatoes and coriander.

*Serves 4–6*

# fresh avocado salad with lime & chillies

see variations page 77

Rich and buttery avocados get a complementary lift from fresh lime juice and chillies in this easy-to-assemble salad. To keep the avocados from discolouring, make the salad right before you want to serve it.

2 ripe avocados, peeled, pitted and sliced
1 tsp fresh lime zest
2 tbsp fresh lime juice
1 tsp brown sugar

1 tbsp olive oil
ground dried ancho or chipotle chilli
salt
fresh flat-leaf parsley sprigs, to garnish

Arrange the avocado slices on a platter. In a small bowl, whisk the lime zest and juice, brown sugar and olive oil together. Drizzle the dressing over the avocados. Sprinkle with ancho chilli and salt to taste. Garnish with parsley. Serve immediately.

*Serves 4*

# jicama salad with fresh mint

see variations page 78

Mellow, pale jicama is a round root vegetable sometimes referred to as the Mexican potato. Unlike the potato, however, jicama is eaten raw and really comes into its own when paired with fresh herbs, chillies, tropical fruits and citrus. It's a staple in Mexican salads and is very crunchy when chilled.

1 large jicama (about 700 g/1½ lb) (or use
　daikon radish sweetened with a little sugar)
150 g (5 oz) diced red pepper
150 g (5 oz) diced yellow pepper
150 g (5 oz) diced green pepper

150 g (5 oz) peeled and diced cucumber
1 large orange, peeled, sliced and sectioned
20 g (²/₃ oz) chopped fresh mint
125 ml (4 fl. oz) fresh lime juice
ground dried ancho or chipotle chilli, to taste

Cut the jicama in half. Peel each half, then cut into quarters. Using a box grater or a food processor fitted with the large grater attachment, grate the jicama and place in a large bowl. Stir in the peppers, cucumber, orange and mint. Drizzle with lime juice and season to taste with dried ancho. Chill until ready to serve.

*Serves 4–6*

# cabbage, radish & coriander relish

see variations page 79

Crisp, colourful and delicious, this coleslaw-like relish goes well with fish tacos, grilled fish fillets, chicken or pork.

340 g (12 oz) finely shredded green cabbage
340 g (12 oz) thinly sliced radishes
80 g (3 oz) finely chopped spring onion
2 tbsp finely chopped fresh coriander

for the dressing:
3 tbsp fresh orange juice
2 tbsp fresh lime juice
2 tbsp vegetable oil
salt and pepper

In a large bowl, combine the cabbage, radishes, spring onion and coriander. In a small bowl, whisk the juices and oil together, then season to taste. Pour over the vegetables and toss to blend. Serve immediately.

*Serves 4–6*

# fiesta slaw

see variations page 80

With its fresh lime, chilli and coriander flavours, this side dish is a wonderful complement to fish tacos, grilled fish and shellfish, chicken or pork.

for the dressing
1 small red onion, thinly sliced
1 small red chilli, minced
grated zest of 1 lime
juice of 2 limes

1 (280-g/10-oz.) package finely shredded
  cabbage or coleslaw mix
20 g (²/₃ oz) chopped fresh coriander
olive oil for drizzling
salt and pepper

Combine the onion, chilli, lime zest and lime juice in a small bowl, tossing to coat all pieces. Cover and refrigerate until ready to use. When ready to serve, place the cabbage and coriander in a large serving bowl. Add the onion mixture. Drizzle with olive oil to just moisten, season with salt and pepper and stir to combine thoroughly. Serve immediately.

*Serves 4*

# grilled prawns & mango salad with chipotle–lime vinaigrette

see variations page 81

Fresh prawns and tropical fruit from Baja on the Pacific or the Yucatán Peninsula in the Caribbean make this seaside salad a hit in hot weather.

for the vinaigrette
1 tinned chipotle chilli in adobo sauce, minced
grated zest of 1 lime
2 tbsp fresh lime juice
20 g (²/₃ oz) chopped fresh coriander
120 ml (4 fl. oz) olive oil, plus more for brushing

450 g (1 lb) peeled and deveined large prawns
salt and pepper
640 g (1½ lb) fresh salad greens
1 large mango, pitted, peeled and sliced

For the vinaigrette, combine the chipotle, lime zest and juice, coriander and olive oil in a small bowl. Set aside.

Preheat the grill. Brush the prawns and mango with olive oil, season to taste and grill on both sides until you have good grill marks and the prawns are opaque, about 1–2 minutes per side. Arrange the salad greens on plates, top with prawns and mango and drizzle with the vinaigrette.

*Serves 4*

# mercado fruit salad with honey-lime dressing

see variations page 82

The walled entrance to the outdoor market in Tepoztlán, near Mexico City, is covered in colourful mosaics with scenes from the ancient Aztecs to Spanish and French colonial days. But what's unique about these mosaics is that they're made with local seeds and beans. On market day, shoppers eat their meals at the mercado, including a fruit salad like this one. Use whatever fruit is in season.

150 g (5 oz) chopped fresh mango or papaya
150 g (5 oz) fresh blueberries
150 g (5 oz) chopped fresh honeydew melon
150 g (5 oz) fresh pineapple chunks
150 g (5 oz) seedless red or green grapes

1 tbsp fresh orange zest
125 ml (4 fl. oz) fresh orange juice
1 tbsp fresh lemon juice
100 g (4 oz) honey
60 ml (2 fl. oz) cup fresh lime juice

Combine the fruits in a large bowl. Stir the orange zest, fresh orange juice and the lemon juice in a small bowl, then pour over the fruit. Toss gently to blend. Cover and refrigerate until ready to serve. Right before serving, whisk the honey and lime juice together in a small bowl, pour over the salad and toss to blend. Serve the salad in glass dishes.

*Serves 4–6*

# aztec vegetable & amaranth salad bowl

see variations page 83

Amaranth is a small, round grain that was a staple food of the ancient Aztecs. It's available in bulk in the health food aisle and, when cooked, can be used like rice or pasta in salads. Quinoa can be substituted for the amaranth, if you wish. Serve this salad right away so the avocado doesn't discolour.

210 g (7½ oz) raw amaranth (or quinoa)
340 g (12 oz) fresh or frozen corn kernels
1 red pepper, stemmed, deseeded and sliced
160 g (6 oz) halved cherry tomatoes
80 g (3 oz) chopped spring onions
1 large avocado, pitted, peeled and sliced
chopped fresh coriander and pepita (toasted
    pumpkin seeds), to garnish

for the dressing
120 ml (4 fl oz) olive oil
1 garlic clove, minced
60 ml (2 fl. oz) fresh lime juice
½ tsp ground dried ancho chilli
salt and pepper to taste

Bring 500 ml (1 pint) of water to the boil in a large saucepan. Add the amaranth and cook, covered, for 15 minutes or until the amaranth is tender. Drain. In a large bowl, combine the cooked amaranth with corn, pepper, tomatoes, spring onions and avocado.

In a small bowl, whisk the olive oil, garlic, lime juice and ancho chilli together. Season to taste. Toss the amaranth mixture with the dressing and garnish with coriander and pumpkin seeds.

*Serves 4–6*

variations

# desert cactus soup

see base recipe page 53

### desert cactus soup with chorizo
Prepare the basic recipe, adding 450 g (1 lb) sliced chorizo to the onion to brown.

### desert cactus soup with avocado
Prepare the basic recipe, garnishing with sliced avocado in addition to the other garnishes.

### desert cactus soup with chicken
Prepare the basic recipe, adding 300 g (10 oz) cooked, shredded chicken to the stock.

### pantry shelf cactus soup
Prepare the basic recipe, using 1 (400-g/14-oz) tin of nopalitos, drained, in place of preparing fresh cactus.

# gazpacho with crèma & fresh coriander

see base recipe page 54

### grilled gazpacho
Grill the tomatoes, slices of red onion and whole red pepper over a
medium-hot grill until you have good grill marks. Chop the tomatoes
and onion. Remove the skin from the pepper and chop. Then prepare the
basic recipe.

### mango & peach gazpacho
Prepare the basic recipe, using 300 g (10 oz) chopped and peeled mango and
300 g (10 oz) chopped and peeled peach in place of tomatoes, cucumber,
pepper, onion and bread. Add 250 ml (½ pint) mango nectar, 250 ml
(½ pint) Chardonnay and 10 fresh lime leaves cut into fine shreds. Omit the
crèma, coriander and garlic and garnish with fresh mint sprigs.

### cucumber & suero de leche gazpacho
Prepare the basic recipe, using an additional 150 g (5 oz) chopped seedless
cucumber in place of the tomatoes and pepper. Stir in 240 ml (8 fl. oz)
buttermilk (suero de leche) right before serving.

### orange-tomato gazpacho
Prepare the basic recipe, adding 250 ml (½ pint) fresh orange juice and
2 teaspoons finely grated orange zest.

variations

# mexican roasted sweetcorn & chilli soup

see base recipe page 57

### mexican roasted tomato soup
Prepare the basic recipe, using chopped tomatoes in place of sweetcorn.

### grilled onion & chilli soup
Prepare the basic recipe, using 320 g (11 oz) grilled onion in place of
sweetcorn.

### sweetcorn & black bean soup
Prepare the basic recipe, using 2 ears of sweetcorn instead of 4. Add
200 g (½ lb) tinned black beans with the chicken stock and proceed with
the recipe.

### roasted sweetcorn, chilli & chicken soup
Prepare the basic recipe, adding 300 g (10 oz) cooked, shredded chicken
during the last minutes of simmering.

### roasted courgette & chilli soup
Prepare the basic recipe, using chopped courgette in place of sweetcorn.

variations

# wild mushroom & chipotle soup

see base recipe page 59

### wild mushroom & crèma soup
Prepare the basic recipe, stirring in 120 ml (4 fl. oz) crèma or sour cream right before serving.

### wild mushroom & roasted sweetcorn soup
Prepare the basic recipe, stirring in 170 g (6 oz) roasted sweetcorn kernels before simmering.

### wild mushroom & toasted cumin soup
Prepare the basic recipe, stirring in 1 teaspoon toasted cumin seeds before simmering. Toast cumin seeds by heating them in a dry frying pan over a high heat until they smell aromatic, about 1 minute. Remove from the heat and add to the soup.

### wild mushroom & chipotle soup with guacamole topper
Prepare the basic recipe. Serve each bowl with a spoonful of authentic guacamole (page 30) in the centre of the soup and garnish with chopped coriander, omitting the sour cream and tomato garnish.

variations

# fresh avocado salad with lime & chillies

see base recipe page 61

### grilled avocado salad with lime & chillies
Halve and pit the avocados, but do not peel. Grill the avocado halves, cut-side down, on a medium-hot barbecue outside or indoors on a griddle pan for 2–3 minutes or until you have good grill marks. Slice and peel the avocado and proceed with the basic recipe.

### orange & avocado salad with lime & chillies
Prepare the basic recipe, adding 1 large orange, cut into small wedges, to the platter.

### tomato & avocado salad with jalapeño dressing
Prepare the basic recipe, adding 160 g (6 oz) cherry tomatoes to the platter and 1 stemmed, deseeded and finely chopped fresh jalapeño to the dressing.

### avocado & grilled prawn salad with lime & chillies
Prepare the basic recipe, adding 450 g (1 lb) grilled large prawns to the platter. To prepare the prawns, brush the peeled and deveined prawns with olive oil and season with salt and pepper. Grill the prawns indoors, turning, on a griddle pan for 2–3 minutes per side or until they have good grill marks and are opaque and cooked through.

variations

# jicama salad with fresh mint

see base recipe page 63

### jicama salad with fresh orange & coriander-lime vinaigrette
Prepare the basic recipe, using 20 g (²/₃ oz) chopped fresh coriander in place
of mint.

### jicama & watermelon salad
Prepare the basic recipe, using 450 g (15 oz) finely chopped watermelon in
place of the red, green and yellow peppers.

### jicama, honeydew & cantaloupe salad
Prepare the basic recipe, using 200 g (7½ oz) finely chopped honeydew
melon and 200 g (7½ oz) finely chopped cantaloupe in place of the red,
green and yellow peppers.

### jicama salad with cucumber & lime
Prepare the basic recipe, using 450 g (15 oz) finely chopped cucumber in
place of the red, green and yellow peppers.

# cabbage, radish & coriander relish

see base recipe page 64

### citrus & herb relish
Prepare the basic recipe, using 150 g (5 oz) fresh orange segments in place of radishes.

### orange & coriander relish
Prepare the basic recipe, using 300 g (10 oz) fresh orange segments in place of the cabbage and radishes.

### mexican sweetcorn relish
Prepare the basic recipe, using 170 g (6 oz) cooked sweetcorn kernels and 150 g (5 oz) diced red pepper in place of the cabbage and radishes.

### carrot, onion & jalapeño relish
Prepare the basic recipe, using 160 g (6 oz) grated carrots and 160 g (6 oz) stemmed, deseeded and diced fresh jalapeño in place of the cabbage and radishes.

variations

# fiesta slaw

see base recipe page 67

### baja slaw
Prepare the basic recipe, using a small green chilli in place of the red.

### coriander slaw
Prepare the basic recipe, using 4 chopped spring onions in place of the red onion and a small green chilli in place of the red.

### mexican slaw with chipotle–lime vinaigrette
Prepare the basic recipe, adding 1 tinned chipotle chilli in adobo sauce, finely chopped, to the dressing.

### hot & spicy slaw
Prepare the basic recipe, adding 1 stemmed, deseeded and chopped fresh habañero chilli to the slaw.

# grilled prawn & mango salad with chipotle–lime vinaigrette

see base recipe page 69

**grilled scallops & mango salad with chipotle–lime vinaigrette**
Prepare the basic recipe, using scallops in place of prawns.

**grilled chicken & pineapple salad with chipotle–lime vinaigrette**
Prepare the basic recipe, using 450 g (1 lb) boneless, skinless chicken breast
in place of prawns and fresh pineapple rings in place of mango.
Grill the chicken for 4 or 5 minutes per side or until 74°C (165°F) in the
thickest part. Chop the chicken and arrange the pieces on the salad.

**grilled swordfish and papaya salad with chipotle–lime vinaigrette**
Prepare the basic recipe, using grilled swordfish steaks in place of prawns
and fresh papaya in place of mango. Grill the swordfish for 4–5 minutes per
side, then chop and arrange on the salad.

**grilled tuna & papaya salad with chipotle–lime vinaigrette**
Prepare the basic recipe, using fresh sashimi-grade tuna in place of prawns
and fresh papaya in place of mango. Sear the tuna over a very high heat,
turning once, until you have good grill marks on both sides but the tuna is
still raw, then chop and arrange on the salad.

variations

# mercado fruit salad with honey–lime dressing

see base recipe page 71

### papaya, mango & lime salad with mango cream
Prepare the basic recipe, using a total of 750 g (1 lb 12 oz) chopped fresh
papaya and mango in place of the mixed fruits; lime zest and juice in
place of orange zest and juice; and mango cream (page 27) in place of
honey–lime dressing.

### grilled citrus salad with honey–lime dressing
Preheat your grill to high. Peel and slice 2 grapefruits, 4 oranges,
2 limes and 2 lemons. Brush the cut sides with vegetable oil. Grill, turning
once, until you have good grill marks, about 1–2 minutes per side. Arrange
on a platter and drizzle with the honey–lime dressing.

### fresh melon salad with honey–lime dressing
Prepare the basic recipe, using 300 g (10 oz) chopped and deseeded fresh
watermelon and 450 g (15 oz) chopped fresh honeydew melon in place of
the mixed fruits.

### mercado berry salad with honey–lime dressing
Prepare the basic recipe, using 450 g (15 oz) fresh blueberries and 300 g
(10 oz) fresh hulled and halved strawberries in place of the mixed fruits.

# aztec vegetable & amaranth salad bowl

see base recipe page 72

### yucatán rainforest platter
Prepare the basic recipe, using 600 g (1 lb 4 oz) chopped tropical fruits in place of the sweetcorn, pepper, cherry tomatoes and spring onions.

### tex-mex grilled vegetable platter
Prepare the basic recipe, grilling the red pepper, cherry tomatoes and spring onions before adding them to the salad.

### mexico city market-day platter
Prepare the basic recipe, adding cooked chorizo to the platter.

### sonoran desert platter
Prepare the basic recipe, adding nopalitos (page 17) or tinned nopalitos to the platter.

# poultry

Poultry has always been a favourite Mexican food.

Usually, poultry is slow-simmered, then picked from

the bone and shredded to use in fillings for burritos,

enchiladas, chilequiles, tamales, tacos or quesadillas.

But it can also be grilled for fajitas or roasted whole.

# oaxacan chicken in mole

see variations page 105

Conquered by the Aztecs in 1482 and by the Spanish in 1522, Oaxaca is a province known for the variety of its moles (sauces made by grinding many ingredients together). Chicken slowly simmered in a spicy mole becomes fall-apart tender as well as uniquely flavoured. Serve this dish over rice.

2 large chickens, about 1.5 kg (3 lb) each, jointed
1 large onion, sliced
4 cloves garlic, chopped
750 ml (1¹/₂ pints) chicken stock
basic mole (page 17)
chopped fresh coriander, to garnish

Place the chicken pieces in a large saucepan. Add the onion, garlic and chicken stock, and bring to the boil. Reduce the heat to simmer. Cook, covered, for 45 minutes or until the chicken is tender and cooked through. Remove the chicken from the stock; set stock aside.

When cool enough to handle, remove skin, fat and bones from the chicken and discard. Cut the chicken meat into large pieces and reserve. Strain the stock, then return it to the pan. Stir in the basic mole and bring to the boil over medium-high heat. Stir in the chicken and heat through. Serve over hot rice, garnished with coriander.

*Serves 6–8*

# chicken barbacoa

see variations page 106

Barbacoa – foods over an indirect fire outdoors – are popular in Mexico. Cabrito (goat) is the choice in the north, lamb in central Mexico and pork in the Yucatán, but everyone loves chicken. Mesquite chips provide a regional "kiss of smoke" flavour.

1 cup mesquite wood chips (or any hardwood
    chips, such as oak)
1 roasting chicken (about 2 kg/4 lb), cleaned,
    with giblets and neck removed
2 tbsp olive oil

1½ tsp garlic powder
1½ tsp black pepper
1 tsp dried aniseed or fennel
1½ tsp ground dried ancho chilli
1 tsp salt, or to taste

Prepare an indirect fire in your barbecue – the coals or heat to one side and no heat on the other side. For a charcoal barbecue, soak the mesquite chips in water in a bowl; drain. For a gas barbecue, place the dry chips in a smoker box or an aluminium foil packet.

Brush the chicken with olive oil. Combine the spices and salt in a small bowl, then sprinkle the chicken all over with the mixture. Place the chicken, breast-side down, on the indirect side, away from the heat. If using a charcoal barbecue, sprinkle the hot coals with the soaked mesquite chips. For a gas barbecue, place the smoker box or foil packet as close as possible to the gas flame. When you see the first wisp of smoke, close the barbecue lid. Cook, covered, for 1 hour, turning the chicken at intervals to brown evenly, until a meat thermometer inserted in the thickest part of the thigh registers 77°C (170°F). The meat should not be at all pink. Serve hot.

*Serves 4*

# chilaquiles

see variations page 107

Ideal for a casual meal, this tortilla chicken casserole with green chilli sauce is comfort food with a twist. In Tijuana, chilaquiles are a favourite breakfast side dish.

600 g (1 lb 4 oz) shredded cooked chicken
salsa verde (page 214)
240 ml (8 fl. oz) Mexican crèma or sour cream
120 ml (4 fl. oz) cup double cream

12 (15-cm/6-in) fresh corn tortillas, cut into
   6-mm (¼-in) wide strips (shop-bought or
   homemade)
450 g (1 lb) grated Mexican cheese, such as
   Monterey Jack or Chihuahua

Preheat the oven to 175°C (350°F/Gas mark 4). Arrange half the chicken in a 23 x 33-cm (9 x 13-in) baking tin. Top with half the salsa verde. Mix the crèma or sour cream and double cream together and spread half over the salsa. Top with half the tortilla strips and half the grated cheese. Repeat the process.

Bake for 45 minutes or until browned and bubbling. To serve, leave to cool slightly, then cut into squares.

*Serves 8*

# chicken enchiladas

see variations page 108

Enchiladas are a Mexican family staple, using common ingredients – prepared salsas, cooked meats, cheese and corn tortillas. They're great for a casual meal or to feed a crowd.

salsa roja (page 23)
260 g (9 oz) grated Monterey Jack or
    Chihuahua cheese
450 g (15 oz) shredded cooked chicken

salt to taste
vegetable oil for frying
12 (12.5 to 15-cm/5- to 6-in) corn tortillas
    (shop-bought or homemade)

Preheat the oven to 230°C (450°F/Gas mark 8). In a medium bowl, mix 60 ml (2 fl. oz) salsa roja and 50 g (2 oz) cheese with the chicken. Season with salt to taste. Coat the bottom of a medium frying pan with oil, and place the pan over a medium-high heat. When the pan is hot, dip each tortilla into the remaining salsa to lightly coat, then fry on both sides until softened. Transfer to a plate. Add more oil when necessary.

Spread out the tortillas on a flat surface and place 50 g (2 oz) of the chicken filling in the centre of each one. Roll up. Place each roll in a 23 x 33-cm (9 x 13-in) baking tin. Spoon the remaining sauce over the rolled tortillas and sprinkle with the remaining cheese. Bake for 20 minutes or until heated through and bubbling.

*Serves 6–8*

# tortilla soup

see variations page 109

With this savoury soup, you get a fiesta of flavours – and colours – all in one bowl.

60 ml (2 fl. oz) vegetable oil
6 (12.5 to 15-cm/5- to 6-in) fresh corn tortillas
    (shop-bought or homemade), cut in half,
    then into 6-mm (¼-in) strips
160 g (6 oz) chopped onion
2 cloves garlic, minced
1 Anaheim, poblano or large jalapeño chilli,
    stemmed, deseeded and chopped
1 l (2 pints) chicken stock

1 (400-g/14-oz.) tin chopped tomatoes, drained
200 g (7½ oz) shredded cooked chicken
salt and pepper to taste
130 g (4½ oz) grated Monterey Jack cheese,
    to garnish
1 ripe avocado, pitted, peeled and sliced,
    to garnish
10 g (⅓ oz) chopped fresh coriander, to garnish

In a large saucepan, heat the oil over medium-high heat. Fry the tortilla strips in batches until crisp and drain on kitchen towels. Add the onion, garlic and chilli to the remaining oil and cook, stirring, until the onion has softened, about 4 minutes. Stir in the stock, tomatoes and chicken, and bring to the boil. Reduce the heat and simmer, covered, for 15 minutes to let the flavours blend.

To serve, divide half the fried tortilla strips among 4 bowls. Ladle in the soup, then garnish with grated cheese, avocado slices, chopped coriander and the remaining tortilla strips.

*Serves 4*

# anticuchos de pollo

see variations page 110

These grilled chicken skewers are delicious street food that you might find at a mercado or market, but they're just as delicious from your own barbecue.

1kg (2 lb) boneless, skinless chicken breasts cut
   into 5-cm (2-in) pieces
6-8 wooden skewers, soaked in water for
   30 minutes and drained
500 ml (1 pint) mango nectar

60 ml (2 fl. oz) spicy barbecue sauce
1 tsp ground dried chipotle chilli
1 tbsp vegetable oil
freshly chopped coriander, to garnish

Thread the chicken onto the skewers, being careful not to crowd the pieces. In a bowl, whisk together the mango nectar, barbecue sauce, chipotle and vegetable oil. Reserve half the mixture and brush the other half over the chicken.

Prepare a medium-hot barbecue. Grill the skewers for 3–5 minutes per side, turning once, until done. Serve over Mexican confetti rice (page 210), drizzle with the remaining sauce and sprinkle with chopped coriander.

*Serves 6–8*

# chicken tamales with yellow mole

see variations page 111

Also known as mole amarillo, the yellowish-orange sauce that accompanies these tamales is very versatile – it's delicious on just about anything.

1 recipe yellow mole (page 18)
200 g (7½ oz) corn masa flour
300 ml (10 fl. oz) chicken stock
150 g (5 oz) shredded cooked chicken

10 dried cornhusks, soaked in water for
   30 minutes and drained

Make the yellow mole, and while it is simmering, make the tortillas. Place the masa flour in a bowl. Stir in the chicken stock to make a soft dough, adding a little more water if necessary. Divide the dough into 10 portions and form each portion into a ball. Place each ball of dough between 2 unopened plastic sandwich bags, then press to a 12.5 or 15-cm (5- or 6-in) round in a tortilla press.

Place 1 tablespoon of yellow mole and 1 tablespoon of shredded chicken in the middle of each tortilla. Fold in the sides and place in the damp cornhusk. Secure the ends with string so that each tamale is completely enclosed in the husk. Arrange the tamales upright in a steamer, not letting them touch the water, and steam for 30 minutes.

To serve, unwrap each tamale and serve with more yellow mole.

*Serves 4–6*

# huevos rancheros

see variations page 112

Before you can have chicken, you have to start with eggs, right? Ranch-style eggs with soft-fried corn tortillas are a popular dish at many Mexican eateries, from cafés to cantinas. Customize this dish with your choice of garnish.

2 tbsp vegetable oil
6 fresh corn or flour tortillas (store-bought or
    homemade, page 15, 16)
6 large eggs

sliced avocado, fresh coriander sprigs, chopped
    spring onions, shredded cheese and lime
    wedges, to garnish
1 recipe salsa cruda (page 21)

Heat the oil over medium-high heat in a large frying pan. When the oil is hot, fry the corn tortillas for about 10 seconds on each side. Drain on kitchen towels. Crack the eggs into the hot oil and fry the eggs to your desired doneness. To serve, place a soft tortilla on each plate and top with an egg and your chosen garnishes. Serve the salsa on the side.

*Serves 3–6*

# mesquite-grilled turkey piñon

see variations page 113

Pair the turkey with this salsa made from piñon nuts – from pine trees in
northern Mexico.

for the salsa
120 g (4 oz) toasted pine nuts
3 hard-boiled large egg yolks
2 tbsp capers, drained
2 tbsp caper juice
240 ml (8 fl. oz) single cream
salt and pepper to taste

1 cup mesquite wood chips (or any hardwood
  chips, such as oak)
4 (170-g/6-oz) turkey breast steaks
olive oil for brushing

To make the salsa, in a blender or food processor, combine the pine nuts, egg yolks, capers,
caper juice and single cream. Blend until smooth. Season with salt and pepper to taste and
set aside.

Prepare a medium-hot barbecue. For a charcoal barbecue, soak the mesquite chips in water in
a bowl; drain. For a gas barbecue, place dry wood chips in a smoker box or an aluminium foil
packet. Brush the turkey steaks with olive oil, and season with salt and pepper to taste.
If using a charcoal barbecue, sprinkle the hot coals with the soaked mesquite chips. For a gas
barbecue, place the smoker box or foil packet as close as possible to the gas flame. When you
see the first wisp of smoke, place the turkey on the barbecue and close the lid. Cook, covered,
for 6 minutes; turn, cover and grill another 7 minutes or until a meat thermometer inserted in
the thickest part registers 77°C (170°F). Serve hot with the salsa.

*Serves 4*

# quail with rose petals

see variations page 114

Laura Esquivel made this hauntingly delicious dish popular in her novel *Like Water for Chocolate*. Use organic or unsprayed red rosebuds, the most fragrant you can find.

4 quail, cleaned, rinsed and patted dry

for the marinade
6 red rosebuds, organic or unsprayed
85 g (3 oz) sliced almonds
2 garlic cloves

2 tbsp unsalted butter
2 tbsp honey
2 tbsp cornmeal (polenta)
2 tbsp aniseed or fennel seed
salt and pepper to taste

Preheat the oven to 200°C (400°F/Gas mark 6).

Tear the petals from the rosebuds and place them in a food processor or blender along with the almonds and garlic. Run on "pulse" to finely chop. In a saucepan over medium heat, melt the butter and honey together. Add the rose mixture, cornmeal and aniseed or fennel seed, and stir until well blended and fragrant. Season to taste.

Place the quail on a baking sheet and brush with half of the mixture. Roast for 20 minutes, baste with the remaining rose mixture and continue roasting until a meat thermometer inserted in the thickest part of the thigh registers 77°C (170°F). The meat should not be at all pink.

*Serves 4*

# soft tacos with duck

see variations page 115

Mexico is part of the fly-over zone for wildfowl of all kinds going south for the winter. You won't find soft tacos with duck on fast-food menus, but you will in hunters' homes.

4 duck breasts, boned
2 tbsp honey
1 clove garlic, minced
1 tbsp fresh lime juice
salt and pepper to taste
8 large flour tortillas, warmed

1 recipe pineapple, mango or papaya salsa
(page 20, 21)
fresh chopped coriander

With a sharp knife, score the fat side of the duck breasts in a cross-hatched pattern. Heat a large frying pan over a medium-high heat. Cook the duck breasts, fat-side down, for 3–4 minutes or until the fat has browned.

In a small bowl, combine the honey, garlic and lime juice. Turn the duck and brush or drizzle with half of this mixture; reserve the rest. Cook the duck until medium-rare, about 3 more minutes. Remove from the heat, season to taste and leave to rest for 5 minutes.

Slice the duck on the diagonal. Place the slices in the centre of each warmed flour tortilla, drizzle with the remaining honey mixture, top with salsa and coriander, roll up and serve.

*Serves 8*

variations

# oaxacan chicken in mole

see base recipe page 85

### turkey in mole
Prepare the basic recipe, using 1 small turkey (about 3 kg/6 lb), cut up,
or 2 turkey breasts, in place of chicken.

### turkey in green mole
Prepare the basic recipe, using 1 small turkey (about 3 kg/6 lb), cut up, or
2 turkey breasts, in place of chicken, and green mole (page 19) in place of basic
mole.

### duck in mole
Prepare the basic recipe, using 1 large duckling (about 2.5 kg/5lb), cut up, in place
of chicken.

variations

# chicken barbacoa

see base recipe page 86

### turkey breast barbacoa
Prepare the basic recipe, using a turkey breast in place of the
roasting chicken.

### duck breast barbacoa
Prepare the basic recipe, using 4 duckling breasts in place of the
roasting chicken.

### chicken wings barbacoa
Prepare the basic recipe, using 2 kg (4 lb) chicken wings in place of the
roasting chicken.

### beef barbacoa
Prepare the basic recipe, using a 1½-kg (3½-lb) boneless beef chuck roast in
place of the roasting chicken and oregano in place of the aniseed or fennel.

variations

# chilaquiles

see base recipe page 88

### turkey chilaquiles
Prepare the basic recipe, using shredded cooked turkey in place of chicken.

### duck chilaquiles
Prepare the basic recipe, using shredded cooked duck in place of chicken.

### prawn chilaquiles
Prepare the basic recipe, using cooked large prawns in place of chicken.

variations

# chicken enchiladas

see base recipe page 90

### vegetarian cheese & chilli enchiladas
Prepare the basic recipe, using salsa verde (page 214) in place of salsa roja
and 400 g (14 oz) grated Monterey Jack cheese combined with 40 g (1½ oz)
tinned chopped green chillies in place of chicken.

### prawn enchiladas
Prepare the basic recipe, using 450 g (15 oz) cooked prawns in place
of chicken.

### beef enchiladas
Prepare the basic recipe, using 450 g (15 oz) shredded cooked beef in place
of chicken.

variations

# tortilla soup

see base recipe page 93

### vegetarian tortilla soup
Prepare the basic recipe, using vegetable stock in place of chicken stock and black beans in place of shredded chicken.

### tortilla soup with grilled prawns
Prepare the basic recipe, using grilled prawns in place of shredded chicken.

### tortilla soup with turkey
Prepare the basic recipe, using shredded cooked turkey in place of chicken.

variations

# anticuchos de pollo

see base recipe page 95

**grilled pork skewers**

Prepare the basic recipe, using pork tenderloin in place of chicken.

**grilled fish skewers**

Prepare the basic recipe, using halibut, monkfish or salmon in place of chicken.

**grilled beef skewers**

Prepare the basic recipe, using beef sirloin in place of chicken.

**grilled prawn skewers**

Prepare the basic recipe, using large, raw, peeled and deveined prawns in place of chicken.

variations

# chicken tamales with yellow mole

see base recipe page 96

### chicken tamales with green mole
Prepare the basic recipe, using green mole (page 19) in place of yellow mole.

### chicken tamales with salsa roja
Prepare the basic recipe, using salsa roja (page 23) in place of the mole sauce.

### chicken tamales with tomatillo salsa
Prepare the basic recipe, using pantry shelf tomatillo salsa (page 20) in place
of yellow mole.

variations

# huevos rancheros

see base recipe page 98

### huevos con queso
Prepare the basic recipe, sprinkling the eggs with cheese as they are frying.

### huevos con cebolla
After frying the corn tortillas, fry 1 finely chopped onion in the oil for about 5 minutes or until soft. Crack the eggs over the onion and continue with the basic recipe.

### chorizo ranchero
Prepare the basic recipe, replacing the eggs with slices of fried chorizo.

### huevos coriander
Prepare the basic recipe and serve with coriander salsa (page 26) in place of salsa cruda.

# mesquite-grilled turkey piñon

see base recipe page 101

### mesquite-grilled chicken piñon
Prepare the basic recipe, using boneless, skinless chicken breasts in place of turkey.

### mesquite-grilled lamb piñon
Prepare the basic recipe, using 4 lamb chops in place of turkey, but grill them only 3 minutes per side.

### mesquite-grilled salmon piñon
Prepare the basic recipe, using a 1-kg (2-lb) salmon fillet in place of turkey, but grill it only 5 minutes per side.

### mesquite-grilled pork piñon
Prepare the basic recipe, using 4 pork chops in place of turkey.

variations

# quail with rose petals

see base recipe page 102

### cornish game hens with rose petals
Prepare the basic recipe, using Cornish game hens in place of the quail.

### chicken breasts with rose petals
Prepare the basic recipe, using bone-in chicken breasts in place of the quail.

### duck legs with rose petals
Prepare the basic recipe, using 8 duck legs in place of the quail.

# soft tacos with duck

see base recipe page 104

### soft tacos with chicken
Prepare the basic recipe, using chicken breasts in place of duck. Do not score.
Cook in 2 tablespoons vegetable oil on both sides, brushing the cooked side
with the honey mixture, until done.

### soft tacos with turkey
Prepare the basic recipe, using 4 turkey breast slices in place of duck.
Do not score. Sauté in 2 tablespoons vegetable oil on both sides, brushing
the cooked side with the honey mixture, until done.

### soft tacos with pheasant
Prepare the basic recipe, using 4 pheasant breasts in place of duck.
Do not score. Sauté in 2 tablespoons vegetable oil on both sides, brushing
the cooked side with the honey mixture, until done.

### nachos with duck
Prepare the basic recipe. Instead of serving on soft tortillas, cut the cooked
duck breast into small pieces and serve on an ovenproof platter of fried
tortilla chips. Add chopped fresh papaya, mango or peach to taste.
Sprinkle with grated Monterey Jack cheese. Place in a 175°C (350°F/Gas mark
5) oven until the cheese melts, then sprinkle with chopped coriander and
serve hot.

# beef

After beef cattle came to Mexico with the

Spanish, large ranches bordering Arizona, New

Mexico and Texas gave rise to a specific cuisine

known as Tex-Mex, which is centred on beef

(simmered and shredded or grilled), flour tortillas,

beans and chillies.

# oak-grilled corner-cut

see variations page 133

Corner-cut is the triangular-shaped roast from the bottom sirloin. To grill it Mexican-style, simply season it with salt and pepper, mop it with Mexican beer and turn it every 10 minutes until medium-rare. It tastes best on a charcoal grill and is delicious served with warm flour tortillas and frijoles refritos (page 209).

1 corner-cut roast (about 1.5 kg/3 lb)
salt and pepper to taste
1 cup oak chips or chunks, soaked in water for
     at least 30 minutes and drained
250 ml (½ pint) Mexican beer

Prepare a medium-hot charcoal barbecue. Season the roast all over with salt and pepper. Pour the beer in a bowl. Place the drained oak chips on the hot coals. When you see the first wisp of smoke from the wood, place the beef on the barbecue. Grill the roast, covered, for about 10 minutes on each side, basting with the beer every 5 minutes. The roast is done when the internal temperature reaches 60°C (140°F). Let the beef rest for 10 minutes, then slice and serve.

*Serves 8–10*

# sizzling skirt steak fajitas

see variations page 134

Either skirt or flank steak makes incredible fajitas. The trick is to marinate the steak first, cook it only until medium-rare then slice thinly on the diagonal. Serve your fajitas with store-bought or homemade flour tortillas, guacamole and pico de gallo.

125 ml (4 fl. oz) Mexican beer
2 tbsp fresh lime juice
1 clove garlic, minced
2 tsp ground cumin
700 g (1½ lb) skirt steak or flank steak

1 large onion, sliced into 2.5-cm (1-in) rounds
1 red pepper, stemmed, deseeded and quartered
vegetable oil for brushing
salt and pepper to taste

In a sealable plastic bag, combine the beer, lime juice, garlic and cumin. Add the steak, seal the bag and toss to cover the meat. Marinate in the refrigerator for at least 1 hour or up to 8 hours.

Prepare a hot barbecue or heat a cast-iron fajita pan on the hob until very hot. Remove the steak from the marinade, pat it dry and discard the marinade. Brush the onion slices, red pepper and steak with vegetable oil. Season to taste. Grill the onion and pepper for 5–7 minutes per side or until charred and softened. Grill the steak for 2½–3 minutes per side for medium-rare. Let the steak rest for 5 minutes, then slice on the diagonal and serve with the grilled vegetables.

*Serves 4*

# slow-braised mexican short ribs in chipotle sauce

see variations page 135

The longer and slower you braise these ribs, the more tender and flavourful they become. Serve with warm flour tortillas and guacamole or green mole (page 16, 30, 19).

2 kg (4 lb) beef short ribs
salt and pepper to taste
2 tbsp vegetable oil
1 large onion, diced

4 cloves garlic, minced
1 small bottle Mexican beer
2 tinned chipotle chillies in adobo sauce,
    chopped

Season the ribs on both sides. Heat the oil in a heavy, large pot over medium-high heat. Brown the ribs on both sides, in batches, about 15 minutes. Transfer the ribs to a plate.

Cook the onion and garlic in the same pot until the onion is translucent, about 5 minutes. Return the ribs to the pot and add the beer and chipotles. Bring to the boil, then reduce the heat. Simmer, covered, until the ribs are tender, about 3 hours.

*Serves 4*

# carne asada in agua negra marinade

see variations page 136

Carne asada is usually a thin beef steak, either cooked on a comal (griddle) indoors or on a barbecue outside. Marinated in a dark mixture of tropical juices, soy sauce and garlic, this steak can be sliced and served as an entrée or used as a filling for burritos and tacos.

80 ml (2½ fl. oz) pineapple juice
2 tbsp fresh lime juice
80 ml (2½ fl. oz) soy sauce
1 clove garlic, minced
2 tsp ground cumin

700 g (1½ lb) flank steak
vegetable oil for brushing
salt and pepper to taste
authentic guacamole (page 30), to garnish
pico de gallo (page 15), to garnish

In a sealable plastic bag, combine the juices, soy sauce, garlic and cumin. Add the steak, seal the bag and toss to cover the meat. Marinate in the refrigerator for at least 1 hour or up to 8 hours.

Prepare a hot barbecue. Remove the steak from the marinade, pat it dry and discard the marinade. Brush the steak with vegetable oil and season to taste. Grill for 2½–3 minutes per side for medium-rare. Let the steak rest for 5 minutes, then slice on the diagonal and serve with guacamole and pico de gallo.

*Serves 4*

# mexican beef brisket stew

see variations page 137

Known as caldillo (little soup), this brothy stew makes great cold weather fare.

2 tbsp vegetable oil
1 kg (2 lb) beef brisket, diced
1 onion, sliced
3 potatoes, peeled and diced
160 g (6 oz) chopped tinned tomatoes, with liquid

3 jalapeño peppers, stemmed, deseeded
    and minced
3 cloves garlic, minced
1 tsp salt
500 ml (1 pint) beef stock

Heat the oil over medium-high heat in a heavy, large pot. Brown the beef and onion for about 10 minutes. Add the potatoes, tomatoes, chillies, garlic, salt and stock. Bring to a boil, then reduce the heat and simmer, covered, for 1–1½ hours or until the beef is tender.

*Serves 6–8*

# grilled steak in salsa roja

see variations page 138

For bold flavour, this steak with its zesty sauce and melted cheese is a winner. Serve with frijoles refritos (page 209) and Mexican confetti rice (page 210).

4 boneless sirloin or rib-eye steaks, cut
    2.5 cm (1 in) thick
vegetable oil for brushing

salt and pepper to taste
salsa roja (page 23)
130 g (4¹/₂ oz) grated Monterey Jack cheese

Prepare a hot barbecue. Brush the steak with vegetable oil and season to taste. Grill for 2¹/₂ minutes on one side. Turn, spoon 1 tablespoon salsa roja on each steak and top each steak with a quarter of the cheese. Close the lid of the grill and grill for 2¹/₂ minutes more or until the cheese has melted and the steak is medium-rare.

*Serves 4*

# mexican pot roast

see variations page 139

Beef chuck, slow-simmered to a tender turn, is made all the more delicious with south-of-the-border seasonings.

2 tbsp vegetable oil
1.5 kg (3 lb) boneless chuck roast
salt and pepper
1 tsp ground cumin
1 large onion, sliced

2 cloves garlic, minced
1 (400-g/14-oz) tin tomatoes with green chillies, with liquid
1 cup any bottled Mexican marinade

Heat the oil over medium-high heat in a large pot. Season the beef on both sides with salt, pepper and cumin. Brown the beef all over for about 10 minutes. Add the onions, garlic, tomatoes and chipotle mojo marinade. Bring to the boil, then reduce the heat and simmer, covered, for 2–2½ hours or until the beef is tender.

*Serves 6-8*

# chilli colorado

see variations page 140

This recipe is the ancestor of chilli con carne. The beef is slow-simmered in a red chilli broth. Serve it with warm flour tortillas to soak it all up.

for the chilli purée
8 dried red chillies, such as guajillo or
    New Mexico
250 ml (½ pint) hot water
2 cloves garlic
1 tsp ground cumin
1 tsp dried oregano leaves
1 (400-g/14-oz) tin chopped tomatoes, with liquid

2 tbsp vegetable oil
1.5 kg (3 lb) boneless chuck roast, cut into
    2.5-cm (1-in) cubes
salt and pepper
1 large onion, sliced
grated Monterey Jack cheese, to garnish
pico de gallo (page 15), to garnish
warm flour tortillas, for serving

On a comal (griddle) over medium-high heat, toast the chillies for 2 minutes on each side. Place the toasted chillies in a bowl and pour the hot water over them. Let the chillies soften for 30 minutes, then stem and seed them, reserving the soaking water. Place the chillies, garlic, cumin, oregano, tomatoes and 60 ml (2 fl. oz) of the soaking water in a food processor or blender. Purée until smooth. Set aside.

Heat the oil over medium-high heat in a heavy, large pot. Season the beef and then brown all over for about 20 minutes. Add the sliced onion and chilli purée. Bring to the boil, then reduce the heat and simmer, covered, for 2–2½ hours or until the beef is tender. Serve in bowls, topped with grated Monterey Jack cheese and pico de gallo, and accompanied by flour tortillas.

*Serves 6-8*

# soft beef tacos with salsa

see variations page 141

Tacos have gone so mainstream that many families have a regular "taco night". Fresh, homemade tortillas make all the difference, as do fresh fillings and accompaniments.

450 g (1 lb) beef mince
160 g (6 oz) chopped onion
2 cloves garlic, minced
2 tbsp taco seasoning
125 ml (4 fl. oz) any bottled Mexican marinade

1 recipe homemade flour tortillas (page 16) or
    soft corn tortillas (page 15), warmed
salsa cruda (page 21)
sour cream, shredded lettuce and grated
    Monterey Jack cheese, to garnish

In a frying pan over a medium-high heat, brown the beef, onion and garlic together. Add the taco seasoning and chipotle mojo marinade. Leave to simmer for 5 minutes.

To serve, place a spoonful of taco meat in the centre of each tortilla. Top with salsa and the accompaniments of your choice, and roll up.

*Serves 4*

# oak-grilled corner-cut

see base recipe page 117

### oak-grilled corner-cut sandwiches
Prepare the basic recipe and slice the steak. Serve it between two slices of grilled bread slathered with your favourite salsa or barbecue sauce.

### oak-grilled corner-cut fajitas
Prepare the basic recipe, slice the steak and then cut it into thin strips. Serve the strips wrapped in a warm flour tortilla with your favourite condiments.

### oak-grilled corner-cut salad
Prepare the basic recipe, slice the steak and then cut it into thin strips. Arrange the strips on top of sliced tomatoes. Top with guacamole and chopped green onions, then serve.

variations

# sizzling skirt steak fajitas

see base recipe page 118

### sizzling chicken fajitas
Prepare the basic recipe, using boneless, skinless chicken breast in place of steak. Grill for 4–5 minutes per side, turning once, or until done.

### sizzling veggie fajitas
Prepare the basic recipe, using portabello mushrooms in place of steak. Marinate for 1 hour, then grill for 2–3 minutes per side or until you have good grill marks.

### sizzling lamb fajitas
Prepare the basic recipe, using boneless lamb shoulder in place of steak.

variations

# slow-braised mexican
# short ribs in chipotle sauce

see base recipe page 121

### slow-braised mexican short ribs in tomato & chilli sauce

Prepare the basic recipe, adding 1 (400-g/14-oz) tin chopped tomatoes
with liquid when you add the beer and chipotles to the pot.

### slow-braised lamb ribs in chipotle sauce

Prepare the basic recipe, using lamb ribs in place of beef.

### slow-braised pork chops in chipotle sauce

Prepare the basic recipe, using pork chops in place of beef short ribs.
Bake for 1 hour, covered, or until the pork chops are tender.

# carne asada in agua negra marinade

see base recipe page 122

### carne asada in mexican beer marinade
Prepare the basic recipe, using Mexican beer in place of soy sauce in the marinade.

### carne asada in lime chipotle marinade
Prepare the basic recipe, using any bottled Mexican marinade in place of soy sauce in the marinade.

### carne asada in margarita marinade
Prepare the basic recipe, using bottled margarita mix in place of soy sauce in the marinade.

### carne asada in pineapple–papaya marinade
Prepare the basic recipe, using papaya nectar in place of soy sauce in the marinade.

variations

# mexican beef brisket stew

see base recipe page 125

### mexican lamb & tomatillo stew
Prepare the basic recipe, using boneless lamb shoulder in place of beef and husked tomatillos in place of tomatoes.

### mexican pork & sweet potato stew
Prepare the basic recipe, using boneless pork shoulder in place of beef and sweet potatoes in place of white potatoes.

### mexican goat stew
Prepare the basic recipe, using boneless goat shoulder in place of beef. Shred the meat and serve with warm flour tortillas.

### mexican game stew
Prepare the basic recipe, using boneless venison roast in place of beef. Shred the meat and serve with warm flour tortillas.

variations

# grilled steak in salsa roja

see base recipe page 127

### grilled steak in green mole
Prepare the basic recipe, using green mole (page 19) in place of salsa roja.

### grilled steak in chipotle sauce
Prepare the basic recipe, using store-bought chipotle sauce in place of
salsa roja.

### grilled steak with cheese & chillies
Prepare the basic recipe, using roasted, chopped poblano chillies on top of
the steak instead of the salsa. Top the chillies with the cheese and serve with
your favourite salsa on the side.

### grilled steak with pumpkin seed salsa
Prepare the basic recipe, replacing the salsa roja with pumpkin seed salsa
(page 25).

variations

# mexican pot roast

see base recipe page 128

### mexican pot roast in a banana leaf
Prepare the basic recipe, omitting the chipotle mojo marinade. Transfer the pot roast and vegetables to the centre of a frozen and thawed banana leaf. Wrap the leaf around the pot roast, place in a pan with the seam down and cook in a 150°C (300°F/Gas mark 2) oven for 2½–3 hours or until the beef is tender.

### mexican beer-braised pot roast
Prepare the basic recipe, using 1 small bottle Mexican beer in place of the Mexican marinade.

### mexican tomato & chilli pot roast
Prepare the basic recipe, adding 1 stemmed, deseeded and chopped fresh jalapeño chilli.

### chipotle pot roast
Prepare the basic recipe, adding 3 tinned and chopped chipotle chillies in adobo, with some of the adobo sauce.

variations

# chilli colorado

see base recipe page 131

### turkey chilli colorado
Prepare the basic recipe, using boneless, skinless turkey in place of the beef.

### chicken chilli colorado
Prepare the basic recipe, using boneless, skinless chicken in place of the beef.

### vegetarian chilli colorado
Prepare the basic recipe, using 1 kg (2 lb) texturized vegetable protein (TVP) or firm tofu in place of the beef. Simmer for 1 hour or until the flavours blend.

### chilli con carne
Prepare the basic recipe, using 1 kg (2 lb) beef mince in place of the cubed beef and adding 1 (400-g/14-oz) can chilli beans. Simmer for 1 hour or until the flavours blend.

variations

# soft beef tacos with salsa

see base recipe page 132

### soft chicken tacos with salsa
Prepare the basic recipe, using ground or finely chopped chicken in place of beef.

### soft pork tacos with salsa
Prepare the basic recipe, using ground pork in place of beef.

### soft seafood tacos with salsa
Prepare the basic recipe, using raw, peeled and deveined prawns in place of beef.

### soft grilled vegetable tacos with salsa
Prepare the basic recipe, using 320 g (11 oz) sliced onions, courgettes and squash in place of beef. Brush the slices with olive oil and grill on both sides until you have good grill marks. Season to taste.

# pork & lamb

Although the Maya and Aztecs hunted wild pigs known as peccaries, domestic pigs and sheep came to Mexico from Spain. Simmered with Mexican seasonings, wrapped in banana leaves and roasted or grilled, pork and lamb have become integral parts of the cuisine.

# pork carnitas

see variations page 160

Shredded carnitas or "little meats", slowly braised in a flavourful stock, are delicious in tacos, burritos, tamales and other dishes.

2.5 kg (5 lb) boneless pork
    shoulder or butt
4 cups chicken stock
1 large onion, quartered
1 tbsp coriander seeds
1 tbsp cumin seeds

1 tsp dried oregano leaves
3 tinned chipotle chillies in
    adobo sauce
2 bay leaves

Place the pork in a large saucepan over a medium-high heat and brown the meat on both sides. Add the stock, onion, seeds, oregano, chipotles and bay leaves, and bring to the boil. Reduce the heat and simmer, covered, until tender and the meat pulls apart from the bone (about 3 hours).

Remove the meat from the pan and leave to cool. Strain, then chill the stock. When the meat is cool enough to handle, remove and discard the fat and any gristle. Skim the fat from the stock. Shred the meat and moisten with a little stock. Serve with rice and beans or as a filling in tacos, burritos, tamales or tostadas.

*Serves 8*

# mayan-style roast pork in banana leaves

see variations page 161

Although the authentic Mayan recipe involved a wild pig known as a peccary, you can approximate the flavour with domestic pork shoulder. Wrapping the meat in a banana leaf keeps the juices in and adds a slightly herbaceous flavour. In place of banana leaves, you can use a paper bag – just put the meat in the bag and fold the open end closed.

2 tbsp salt
2 tbsp pepper
2 tbsp granulated garlic
2 tbsp ground dried chipotle chilli

1 (1.5–2-kg/3–4-lb) boneless pork shoulder
frozen banana leaves, thawed
225 g (8 oz) queso fresco, crumbled, to garnish
chopped fresh coriander, to garnish

Prepare an indirect fire in your barbecue (the coals or heat to one side and no heat on the other side). Combine the salt, pepper, granulated garlic and dried chipotle. Rub this mixture into the surface of the meat. Place the pork on the indirect side of the barbecue, cover and cook for 3 hours. Remove. Place the pork in the centre of a thawed banana leaf section. Wrap the pork and put it in a roasting tin, seam-side down. Cook in a 120°C (250°F) oven for 2½–3 hours or until tender.

To serve, unwrap the meat and shred it, removing fat and gristle. Serve, garnished with queso fresco and chopped coriander.

*Serves 6–8*

# chorizo with eggs & potatoes

see variations page 162

Known as *chorizo con huevos y papas*, this breakfast dish is a favourite at many basic eateries. Made with shredded or finely chopped pork seasoned with smoked, dried chillies, chorizo has a reddish colour and a spicy flavour. The sultanas add a touch of sweetness to counter the spicy chorizo.

2 tbsp vegetable oil
160 g (6 oz) chopped onions
2 large baking potatoes, peeled and finely chopped
225g (½ lb) chorizo sausage

3 tbsp golden sultanas, soaked in hot water for 30 minutes
8 large eggs
chopped fresh coriander, to garnish
warm corn tortillas, for serving

In a large frying pan, heat the vegetable oil over a medium-high heat. Add the onions and potatoes and fry, stirring, for 10 minutes. Add the chorizo and cook, stirring to break up the sausage, until the onions and potatoes begin to turn brown. Stir in the sultanas. Crack the eggs into the pan, one at a time, and cook them on top of the sausage and vegetables, until the eggs are done. Garnish with chopped coriander. Serve with warm corn tortillas.

*Serves 4*

# costillar asado

see variations page 163

Seasoned with oregano and garlic, slathered with salsa roja, grilled until tender, then finished with a sweet touch of honey, these succulent ribs are delicious washed down with Mexican beer.

2 tbsp salt
2 tbsp pepper
2 tbsp granulated garlic
2 tbsp dried oregano

2 racks baby back ribs
1 recipe salsa roja (page 23)
170 g (6 oz) honey

Prepare a medium-hot barbecue. Combine the salt, pepper, garlic and oregano. Season the ribs all over with this mixture. Brush the ribs with half the salsa roja. Grill, turning often, until the meat begins to pull back from the ends of the bone, about 45 minutes. Drizzle the honey over the ribs and continue to grill, turning often, for 15 more minutes. Serve with the remaining salsa roja.

*Serves 8*

# pork & green chilli pozole

see variations page 164

Pozole, a stewlike dish made with hominy and pork, is special-occasion fare in Mexico. It's especially loved in Guerrero State on the southern Pacific Coast, where restaurants called pozolerias offer their signature versions. Pozole is considered a good cure for hangovers and is often eaten in the early hours after a night on the town.

750 g – 1 kg (1½–2 lb) boneless pork shoulder
2 cups tinned white or yellow hominy, drained
4 cloves garlic, minced
6 cups chicken stock
1 cup toasted, shelled pumpkin seeds (pepitas)

1 (380-g/13-oz) can tomatillos, with liquid
1 jalapeño pepper, stemmed and deseeded
20 g (⅔ oz) chopped fresh coriander
fresh avocado slices and lime wedges, to garnish

Place the pork, hominy, garlic and broth in a large pot over a medium-high heat. Bring to the boil, then simmer, covered, for 1½–2 hours or until the pork is tender. Transfer the pork to a plate and leave to cool slightly. Let the stock cool in the pot.

In a blender or food processor, process the pumpkin seeds until fine, then add the tomatillos, jalapeño and coriander. Process until smooth, then set aside.

Shred the pork, removing any fat and gristle. Skim off any fat from the stock and return the meat to the pot. Bring the pozole to a boil again, then reduce the heat. Stir the pepita mixture into the pozole and simmer for 30 minutes. Serve hot in bowls, garnished with avocado slices and lime wedges.

*Serves 4–6*

# pork & poblano tamales

see variations page 165

Because tamales are easy but labour-intensive, they're usually made when families have gathered for holidays or special occasions. They're also made for fundraisers in Mexican communities.

200 g (8 oz) lard or white vegetable fat
325 g (11 oz) corn masa flour
1 tsp salt
2–2$^1\!/_2$ cups hot chicken stock
24 dried cornhusks, soaked for 30 minutes in boiling water, drained

for the filling
5 poblano chillies, roasted, stemmed, deseeded and diced
300 g (10 oz) cooked, shredded pork carnitas (page 143) or pork shoulder
20 g ($^2\!/_3$ oz) finely chopped fresh coriander

To make the dough for the tamales, beat the lard in a large bowl with an electric mixer until light and fluffy, about 3 minutes. Place the corn masa flour and salt in another large bowl, pour the hot stock over and stir until you have a soft dough. Beat the masa dough into the lard, a little at a time, until the dough is light and airy.

For the filling, combine the poblanos, pork and coriander in a medium bowl.

Arrange the cornhusks on a flat surface. Spread about one-twelfth of the dough onto the bottom half of each tamal. Place about 1 tablespoon of the filling on the dough. Fold the sides in, then the ends, to enclose the filling. Place the tamales vertically in a steamer; do not let them touch the water. Steam for 45-60 minutes or until the husks pull away from the filling. Serve.

*Serves 12*

# pork chops in green mole

see variations page 166

The natural sweetness of pork gets a kiss of smoke from the grill and a tangy green finishing sauce from the Puebla region in south-central Mexico. A medium barbecue will give your pork chops good grill marks and a delicious juicy flavour.

4 boneless pork chops, cut 2.5-cm (1-in) thick
1 recipe green mole (page 19)
vegetable oil for brushing

salt and pepper
crèma or sour cream and coriander sprigs, to garnish

In a sealable plastic bag, place the pork chops and half the mole. Seal the bag and toss to cover the meat. Marinate in the refrigerator for at least 1 hour or up to 8 hours.

Prepare a medium barbecue. Remove the chops from the marinade, pat them dry and discard the marinade. Brush the chops with vegetable oil and season to taste. Grill for 10 minutes per side, turning once. Serve each chop with the remaining mole, a dollop of crèma and a sprig of coriander.

*Serves 4*

# guava-glazed leg of lamb

see variations page 167

The state of Michoacan on the Pacific coast is noted for its guavas – sweet and aromatic tropical fruits that originated in southern Mexico.

500 g (¹/₂ lb) guava jelly (or use a mix of
   pineapple and strawberry preserves)
4 cloves garlic, minced
2 tbsp fresh lime juice

60 ml (2 fl. oz) tequila
1 leg of lamb (about 1.5–2 kg/3-4 lbs), boned
   and tied

For the glaze, whisk the guava jelly and garlic together in a saucepan over a medium heat until the jelly has melted and the flavours have blended. Remove from the heat and stir in the lime juice and tequila.

Prepare an indirectly heated barbecue – the coals or heat to one side and no heat on the other side. Brush the lamb with half the glaze. Place the lamb on the indirect side, cover and cook for 1 hour. Turn the lamb over and baste with the remaining glaze.
Cover and continue to cook until a meat thermometer in the thickest part reads 57–60°C (135-140°F) for medium-rare. To serve, let the lamb rest for 10 minutes, then carve into slices.

*Serves 6–8*

# braised lamb shanks
# with tequila & chillies

see variations page 168

Braise the lamb shanks in their south-of-the-border stock until meltingly tender, then enjoy them with Mexican confetti rice (page 210) and slow-simmered black beans (page 208).

2 tbsp vegetable oil
4 lamb shanks
160 g (6 oz) chopped onion
2 cloves garlic, minced
160 g (6 oz) chopped, tinned tomatoes, drained
2 tinned chipotle chillies in adobo sauce, diced,
    with some of the adobo sauce

125 ml (4 fl. oz) brewed coffee
2 tbsp crumbled brown sugar
125 ml (4 fl. oz) tequila
salt and pepper
fresh coriander sprigs, to garnish

Heat the oil in a large pot over a medium-high heat. Add the lamb shanks and brown on all sides, for about 10 minutes. Transfer the shanks to a plate and sauté the onion and garlic for about 4 minutes, or until transparent. Add the tomatoes, chillies, coffee, sugar and tequila, and cook, stirring, until the sugar melts. Return the lamb shanks to the pot and bring to the boil. Reduce the heat and simmer, covered, until the lamb is fork-tender, about $2\frac{1}{2}$–3 hours. Season to taste. Serve with the sauce, garnishing each plate with coriander sprigs.

*Serves 4*

# veracruz-style grilled leg of lamb

see variations page 169

Veracruz is known for its sugarcane, citrus and tropical fruits, avocados, coffee and vanilla. Foods cooked in the Veracruz style usually include fresh citrus, and this lamb is a delicious example. Achiote is a packaged seasoning and food dye made from annatto seeds; it is available in the Hispanic section of the supermarket.

for the seasoning
2 tbsp prepared achiote
1 tsp black pepper
1 tsp salt
1 tbsp freshly grated orange zest
3 tbsp fresh orange juice
2 tbsp vegetable oil

1 boned and butterflied leg of lamb,
    about 1.5–2 kg (3-4 lb)
warm flour tortillas (store-bought or homemade
    page 16), for serving
fresh guacamole with lime & garlic (page 44),
    for serving

In a small bowl, mix the achiote with the pepper, salt, orange zest, juice and oil. Brush mixture all over the lamb. Leave to rest at room temperature for 1 hour.

Prepare an indirectly heated barbecue – the coals or heat to one side and no heat on the other. Place the lamb on the indirect side, cover and grill for 1½–2 hours or until a meat thermometer inserted in the thickest part shows 57–60°C (135-140°F) for medium-rare.

To serve, let the lamb rest for 10 minutes, then carve into slices. Serve with warm flour tortillas and guacamole.

*Serves 6–8*

variations

# pork carnitas

see base recipe page 143

### lamb carnitas
Prepare the basic recipe, using boneless lamb shoulder in place of pork.
Serve topped with crumbled queso fresco and chopped fresh mint.

### cabrito carnitas
Prepare the basic recipe, using boneless cabrito shoulder in place of pork.
Serve on mini corn or flour tortillas drizzled with a little smoky barbecue
sauce for a Tex-Mex starter.

### beef carnitas
Prepare the basic recipe, using boneless beef chuck in place of pork.
Serve this on a bolillo or hard roll, with your favourite toppings, as a torta
or sandwich.

variations

# mayan-style roast pork in banana leaves

see base recipe page 144

### mayan-style roast chicken in banana leaves
Prepare the basic recipe, using a whole roasting chicken in place of pork.
Indirect grill for 1 hour, then wrap in banana leaves (a large paper bag
makes a good substitue for banana leaves – just put the meat in the bag
and fold the open end closed) and finish in the oven for 1 more hour.

### mayan-style roast whole fish in banana leaves
Prepare the basic recipe, using a whole, cleaned fish in place of pork. Rub it
with the seasoning mixture, then wrap in banana leaves and indirect grill for
1½ hours or until the fish flakes when tested with a fork.

### mayan-style roast lamb in banana leaves
Prepare the basic recipe, using 4 racks of lamb ribs in place of pork.
Indirect grill for 2 hours, then wrap in banana leaves and finish in the oven
for 1 more hour.

### mayan-style roast goat in banana leaves
Prepare the basic recipe, using 1 leg of goat in place of pork. Indirect grill for
2 hours, then wrap in banana leaves and finish in the oven for 2 more hours
or until tender.

variations

# chorizo with eggs & potatoes

see base recipe page 146

### pork carnitas with eggs & potatoes
Prepare the basic recipe, using pork carnitas (page 143) in place of chorizo and chopped fresh green chillies in place of the sultanas.

### costillar asado with eggs & potatoes
Why not serve leftover spare ribs for breakfast? Prepare the basic recipe, omitting the chorizo and sultanas. Warm the spare ribs (page 148) in the oven. Serve on the side, as you would breakfast sausage or bacon.

### carne asada with eggs & potatoes
Have some leftover steak for breakfast. Prepare the basic recipe, omitting the chorizo and sultanas. Warm the carne asada (page 122) in the microwave or a hot frying pan to accompany the eggs and potatoes.

variations

# costillar asado

see base recipe page 148

### mexican barbecued beef ribs
Prepare the basic recipe, using beef ribs in place of baby backs and ground chipotle in place of oregano. Marinate the ribs in Mexican beer for up to 12 hours, then pat dry, season and grill as directed.

### mexican barbecued lamb ribs
Prepare the basic recipe, using lamb ribs in place of baby backs. Marinate the lamb ribs in pineapple juice for up to 2 hours, then pat dry, season and grill as directed.

### mexican barbecued goat ribs
Prepare the basic recipe, using goat ribs in place of baby backs. Marinate the ribs in bottled Mexican marinade for up to 2 hours, then pat dry, season and grill as directed.

variations

# pork & green chilli pozole

see base recipe page 150

### chicken & green chilli pozole
Prepare the basic recipe, using 2.5 kg (5 lb) cut-up chicken in place of pork.

### lamb & green chilli pozole
Prepare the basic recipe, using boneless lamb shoulder in place of pork.

### turkey & green chilli pozole
Prepare the basic recipe, using 2.5 kg (5 lb) turkey legs in place of pork.

### goat & green chilli pozole
Prepare the basic recipe, using 2.5 kg (5 lb) goat leg in place of pork.

variations

# pork & poblano tamales

see base recipe page 153

### chilli & cheese tamales
Prepare the basic recipe, using cream cheese in place of pork.

### turkey picadillo tamales
Prepare the basic recipe, using turkey empanadas filling (page 51) in place of
the pork filling.

### fresh sweetcorn tamales
Prepare the basic recipe, using fresh sweetcorn kernels in place of pork.

### tamales rapidos
Prepare the basic recipe, using 24 (15-cm/6-in) squares of aluminium foil in
place of soaked and drained cornhusks.

variations

# pork chops in green mole

see base recipe page 154

### pork chops in yellow mole
Prepare the basic recipe, using yellow mole (page 18) in place of green mole.

### pork chops in chipotle sauce
Prepare the basic recipe, using chipotle sauce in place of green mole.
To make the sauce, blend 240 ml (8 fl. oz) tomato-based barbecue sauce
with 2 finely chopped tinned chipotle chillies in adobo sauce and 250 ml
(½ pint) Mexican beer.

### pork chops in pumpkin seed salsa
Prepare the basic recipe, using pumpkin seed salsa (page 25) in place of
green mole.

### pork chops in doctored mole
Prepare the basic recipe, using doctored mole (page 19) in place of
green mole.

# guava-glazed leg of lamb

see base recipe page 156

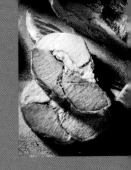

### pineapple-glazed leg of lamb
Prepare the basic recipe, using pineapple preserves in place of guava jelly. Serve with pineapple salsa (page 20).

### margarita-glazed leg of lamb
Prepare the basic recipe, using margarita jelly in place of guava jelly. Garnish with fresh lime and orange.

### mango-glazed leg of lamb
Prepare the basic recipe, using mango jelly (or peach preserve) in place of guava jelly. Serve with mango and lime salsa (page 22).

### prickly pear–glazed leg of lamb
Prepare the basic recipe, using prickly pear cactus jelly (or pear preserve) in place of guava jelly.

variations

# braised lamb shanks with tequila & chillies

see base recipe page 157

### braised lamb shanks in mexican beer
Prepare the basic recipe, using Mexican beer in place of tequila.

### wine-braised lamb shanks
Prepare the basic recipe, using dry red wine in place of tequila.

### braised lamb shanks in mexican chocolate
Prepare the basic recipe, using Mexican hot chocolate (page 270) in place of brewed coffee.

### sangria-braised lamb shanks
Prepare the basic recipe, using sangria (page 263) in place of tequila and 2 jalapeños in place of tinned chipotle chillies in adobo sauce.

# veracruz-style grilled leg of lamb

see base recipe page 159

### tex-mex-style grilled leg of lamb
Prepare the basic recipe, using 240 ml (8 fl. oz) bottled ranch dressing in place of the vegetable oil, orange zest and orange juice, and adding 1 teaspoon ground cumin and 1 teaspoon ground dried ancho chilli to the marinade.

### baja-style grilled leg of lamb
Prepare the basic recipe, using lime zest and lime juice in place of the orange zest and juice.

### oaxaca-style grilled leg of lamb
Prepare the basic recipe, using basic mole (page 17) in place of the marinade.

### guadalajara-style grilled leg of lamb
Prepare the basic recipe, replacing the marinade with a mixture of 60 ml (2 fl. oz) red wine vinegar, 60 ml (2 fl. oz) olive oil, 1 teaspoon ground cumin, 1 tablespoon ground dried ancho chilli, 1 teaspoon dried oregano and salt and pepper to taste.

# fish & shellfish

From the warm waters of the Gulf of Mexico and the Caribbean to the chillier waters of the Pacific, Mexico is blessed with miles of coastline and a wealth of fish and shellfish: prawns, red snapper and grouper from the Gulf and langoustines or lobsters, flounder, swordfish, tuna and yellow snapper from the Pacific.

# mexican seafood stew

see variations page 188

Pescado (fish) and mariscos (shellfish) from both the Gulf and Pacific Coasts of Mexico go into this one-dish meal known as zarzuela.

120 ml (4 fl. oz) vegetable oil
320 g (11 oz) chopped onion
20 g (²/₃ oz) chopped fresh flat-leaf parsley
210 g (7½ oz) long- or short-grain rice
1 (400-g/14-oz) can chopped tomatoes,
    with liquid
250 ml (½ pint) clam juice
250 ml (½ pint) water

10 g (⅓ oz) chopped fresh coriander
450 g (1 lb) boneless, skinless fish fillets, such
    as halibut, grouper or monkfish, cut into
    2.5-cm (1-in) pieces
225 g (½ lb) small bay scallops
225 g (½ lb) large uncooked prawns, peeled and
    deveined
fresh avocado slices and lime wedges, to garnish

Heat the oil in a large pot over medium-high heat. Sauté the onion, stirring, until transparent, about 5 minutes. Stir in the parsley and rice and cook, stirring, until the rice begins to brown. Stir in the tomatoes, clam juice and water. Bring to the boil, then reduce the heat, cover and simmer for 15 minutes. Reduce the heat to low and stir in the coriander, fish, scallops and shrimp. Cover and cook for 10 minutes or until fish and shellfish are opaque. Serve in bowls, garnished with avocado slices and lime wedges.

*Serves 4*

# baja fish tacos

see variations page 189

With a pitcher of margaritas or a frosty Mexican beer, enjoy the fresh flavour of these grilled fish tacos and all the authentic Baja trimmings: red cabbage slaw, pico de gallo and avocado cream. Use whatever mild, white-fleshed fish is freshest.

<sup>1</sup>/<sub>2</sub> head red cabbage, cored and thinly sliced
2 tbsp white wine vinegar
salt and pepper
2 ripe avocados, peeled and pitted
120 ml (4 fl. oz) sour cream
2 tbsp fresh lime juice

6 skinless mahi mahi, pompano, yellow snapper,
    halibut or cod fillets
vegetable oil for brushing
warm flour tortillas, for serving
pico de gallo (page 15), for serving

For the red cabbage slaw, combine the red cabbage and vinegar in a medium bowl and season to taste. For the avocado cream, purée the avocado, sour cream and lime juice in a food processor or blender; season to taste.

Prepare a hot barbecue. Brush the fish with vegetable oil, then season to taste. Measure how thick the fish is in the thickest part (it's usually about 18 mm/³/₄ in). Grill the fish, turning once, for 10 minutes per 2.5 cm (1 in) of thickness (about 7¹/₂ minutes for an 8-mm/³/₄-in thick fillet).

To serve, cut the fish into strips and place in tortillas, garnished with the slaw, avocado cream and pico de gallo.

*Serves 6*

# grilled margarita-glazed fish

see variations page 190

Margaritas are delicious for drinking, but they're also great as a marinade and glaze for fish, shellfish and chicken on the grill.

250 ml (¹/₂ pint) margarita (page 255)
6 skinless mahi mahi, pompano, halibut or
    cod fillets

vegetable oil for brushing
salt and pepper

Place the fish fillets on a baking sheet and brush with half the margarita. Leave to sit at room temperature for 30 minutes.

Prepare a hot barbecue. Brush the fish with vegetable oil, then season to taste. Measure how thick the fish is in the thickest part (it's usually about 18 mm/³/₄ in). Grill the fish, turning once and basting with the remaining margarita, for 10 minutes per 2.5 cm (1 in) of thickness (about 7¹/₂ minutes for an 8-mm/³/₄-in thick fillet).

*Serves 6*

# grilled prawn skewers borrachos

see variations page 191

Marinated in Mexican beer – hence the "drunken" or borrachos in the title – then grilled to perfection, these skewers can be served with Mexican confetti rice (page 210), slow-simmered black beans (page 208) and authentic guacamole (page 30).

1 small bottle Mexican beer
3 cloves garlic, minced
2 tbsp fresh lime juice
450 g (1 lb) large prawns, peeled and deveined

8 wooden skewers, soaked in water for at least 30 minutes and drained
vegetable oil for brushing
salt and pepper

Place the beer, garlic and lime juice in a sealable plastic bag. Add the prawns. Seal the bag and leave to marinate for 30–60 minutes in the refrigerator. Remove the prawns from the bag and thread onto the skewers without crowding; discard the marinade. Brush the prawns with vegetable oil and season to taste.

Prepare a medium-hot barbecue. Grill the skewers for 2–3 minutes per side or until the prawns are opaque and have good grill marks. Place 2 skewers on each serving plate.

*Serves 4*

# grilled fish tostadas with pineapple–lime salsa

see variations page 192

A tostada is a flour tortilla layered with different ingredients, like a pizza.

300 g (10 oz) chopped fresh pineapple
2 tbsp fresh lime juice
$^{1}/_{4}$ tsp dried crushed red chilli flakes
4 (23- to 25-cm/9- to 10-in) flour tortillas, homemade (page 16) or store-bought
vegetable oil for frying and brushing

4 white-fleshed fish fillets, such as mahi mahi, halibut, monkfish or cod
1 tsp ground dried ancho or chipotle chilli
salt and pepper
1 recipe avocado cream (page 172)
100 g (4 oz) shredded lettuce

For the salsa, combine the pineapple, lime juice and red chilli flakes in a bowl. Cover and refrigerate.

For the tostadas, heat 1.2 cm ($^{1}/_{2}$ in) of vegetable oil in a large frying pan over a medium-high heat. Fry the flour tortillas, one at a time, until golden brown on both sides. Transfer to kitchen towels to drain and cool.

Prepare a hot barbecue. Brush the fish fillets with oil and season with ancho chilli, salt and pepper. Measure how thick the fish is at the thickest part (it's usually about 18 mm/$^{3}/_{4}$ in). Grill the fish, turning once, for 10 minutes per 2.5 cm (1 in) of thickness (about 7$^{1}/_{2}$ minutes for an 18-mm/$^{3}/_{4}$-in thick fillet). To serve, spread each tostada with avocado cream and sprinkle with 25 g (1 oz) shredded lettuce. Top with a fish fillet and a quarter of the salsa.

*Serves 4*

# banana leaf-wrapped fish fillets on the grill

see variations page 193

Leaf-wrapping foods is an ancient rainforest cooking method that was popular with both Mayan and Incan cultures. The leaves allow the fish to stay moist, delicious and gently flavoured. You can find banana leaves, fresh and frozen in some large supermarkets and specialist shops. Serve these fillets with slow-simmered black beans (page 208) and Mexican confetti rice (page 210).

1 frozen and thawed banana leaf, cut into 4
    pieces
4 (160-g/6-oz) mahi mahi, halibut, monkfish or
    salmon fillets

salt and pepper
250 ml (½ pint) salsa of your choice

Lay each piece of banana leaf on a flat surface. Place a fish fillet in the centre. Season to taste and top with a quarter of the salsa. Carefully wrap the fish with the banana leaf.

Prepare a medium-hot barbecue or preheat the oven to 175°C (350°F/Gas mark 5). Place the banana leaf parcels on the barbecue or in the oven, close the lid or the door and leave to cook for 16–20 minutes or until the fish flakes when tested with a fork. Remove from the grill or oven. Serve, allowing each diner to unwrap his or her own serving at the table.

*Serves 4*

# tequila lime-grilled scallops

see variations page 194

With a brush of a margarita-like baste, sweet and meaty scallops take on fiesta flavour.

24 large sea scallops

for the marinade
120 ml (4 fl. oz) olive oil
125 ml (4 fl. oz) tequila
125 ml (4 fl. oz) fresh lime juice

1 tsp freshly grated lime zest
2 shallots, finely chopped
2 garlic cloves, minced
2 tsp ground cumin
salt and pepper

Rinse the scallops and pat dry. In a bowl, combine the olive oil, tequila, lime juice, zest, shallots, garlic and cumin. Season to taste. Place the scallops in a sealable plastic bag with half the tequila marinade. Reserve the other half. Seal the bag and shake to blend. Leave to marinate in the refrigerator for 30–60 minutes.

Prepare a hot barbecue or grill. Remove the scallops from the marinade and grill, turning once, for 2–3 minutes per side or until opaque and with good grill marks. Serve drizzled with the remaining marinade.

*Serves 6–8*

# lobster tacos with yellow tomato salsa

see variations page 195

Warm lobster tails on the grill outdoors or in a grill pan inside, then chop up the sweet meat and enjoy a taco vibrant with flavour, colour and texture.

for the salsa
320 g (12 oz) halved small yellow tomatoes or
    diced large yellow tomatoes
2 serrano chillies, stemmed, deseeded and diced
40 g (1½ oz) finely chopped spring onion
225 g (8 oz) frozen and thawed lobster tails,
    shells removed

vegetable oil for brushing
salt and pepper
100 g (4 oz) finely shredded lettuce
180 g (6 oz) guacamole (homemade, page 30,
    or store-bought)
8 packaged taco shells

For the salsa, combine the tomatoes, chillies and spring onion in a bowl, and set aside.

Prepare a medium-hot barbecue or heat a grill pan over a high heat indoors. Brush the lobster tails with vegetable oil and season to taste. Grill for 2–3 minutes per side or until they have good grill marks. Remove the lobster tails and chop the meat.

Portion the lettuce among the taco shells, then top with a dollop of guacamole and some of the warm lobster meat. Serve with the salsa.

*Serves 4*

# camarones a la diabla

see variations page 196

Hot and spicy, this devilled prawns dish makes great party food, served over steamed white rice.

2 ancho or poblano chillies, stemmed and
   deseeded
1 Anaheim chilli, stemmed and deseeded
2 serrano chillies, stemmed and deseeded
320 g (12 oz) chopped tinned tomatoes, with liquid
3 tbsp oil
3 tbsp butter
1/2 onion, thinly sliced lengthways

4 cloves garlic, minced
2 kg (4 lb) large uncooked prawns, peeled
   and deveined
1 tbsp Worcestershire sauce
2 tbsp chicken stock
60 ml (2 fl. oz) white wine
salt and pepper

Place the chillies in a saucepan with enough water to cover. Bring to the boil, then reduce the heat and simmer until tender, about 5 minutes. Drain and place the chillies in a food processor or blender with the tomatoes. Purée and set aside.

In a large pot, heat the oil and butter over medium-high heat. Sauté the onion and garlic until transparent, about 4 minutes. Add the prawns and sauté until just barely pink and opaque, about 3 minutes. Stir in the Worcestershire sauce, chicken stock, wine and tomato-chilli purée, then season to taste and bring to a simmer. Serve over steamed white rice.

*Serves 6-8*

# red snapper veracruzano

see variations page 197

Dishes in the Veracruz style often feature capers, tomatoes and olives – a signature style that blends Spanish seasonings with local Mexican ingredients.

4 red snapper, mahi mahi or halibut fillets
    (about 200 g/8 oz each)
1 recipe salsa cruda (page 21) or 500 ml (1 pint)
    store-bought fresh salsa
$^1/_4$ tsp ground white pepper

1 tsp ground cinnamon
100 g (4 oz) sliced pimiento-stuffed olives
60 ml (2 fl. oz) olive oil
capers, to garnish

Preheat the oven to 200°C (400°F/Gas mark 6). Place the fish fillets in a baking dish. In a bowl, combine the salsa, white pepper, cinnamon, olives and olive oil. Spoon this mixture over the fish. Bake for 15 minutes or until the fish is just beginning to flake.

To serve, place the fish and sauce on plates and garnish with capers.

*Serves 4*

variations

# mexican seafood stew

see base recipe page 171

### shellfish stew in coriander–saffron
Prepare the basic recipe, adding 1 teaspoon saffron threads to the water and using fresh clams or mussels in place of fish. (Do not use any clams or mussels that have opened before cooking and discard any that do not open after cooking.)

### seafood stew with squash, tomatoes & saffron
Prepare the basic recipe, adding 1 teaspoon saffron threads to the water and 150 g (5 oz) diced courgette or squash with the seafood.

### seafood stew in roasted poblano broth
Prepare the basic recipe, adding 160 g (6 oz) roasted, stemmed, deseeded and chopped poblano chilli to the stock after browning the rice.

### smoky mexican seafood stew
Prepare the basic recipe, adding 60 ml (2 fl. oz) bottled smoked chipotle sauce when you add the coriander, fish, scallops and prawns.

variations

# baja fish tacos

see base recipe page 172

### baja prawn tacos
Prepare the basic recipe, using grilled prawns in place of fish.

### baja chicken tacos
Prepare the basic recipe, using slices of grilled, boneless, skinless chicken breasts in place of fish.

### baja swordfish tacos
Prepare the basic recipe, using grilled swordfish steaks seasoned with smoked paprika in place of fish.

### baja vegetarian tacos
Prepare the basic recipe, using grilled tofu in place of fish.

variations

# grilled margarita-glazed fish

see base recipe page 174

### grilled margarita-glazed fish with salsa fresca
Prepare the basic recipe, then serve with a fresh salsa made with 300 g
(10 oz) chopped mango or papaya, 2 tablespoons fresh lime juice and
$\frac{1}{2}$ teaspoon dried red chilli flakes.

### grilled margarita-glazed fish with grilled guacamole
Prepare the basic recipe, then serve with grilled guacamole (page 44).

### grilled margarita-glazed fish with coriander salsa
Prepare the basic recipe, then serve with coriander salsa (page 26)

### grilled margarita-glazed fish with tomatillo salsa
Prepare the basic recipe, then serve with tomatillo salsa (page 19).

### grilled margarita-glazed pork with pineapple salsa
Prepare the basic recipe, using pork chops in place of fish fillets. Serve with
pineapple salsa (page 20).

# grilled prawn skewers borrachos

see base recipe page 176

### grilled prawn skewers in margarita marinade
Prepare the basic recipe, using 250 ml (½ pint) world's best margarita (page 255) in place of the beer, garlic and lime juice marinade. Marinate for only 30 minutes, then grill.

### grilled prawn skewers in citrus mojo
Prepare the basic recipe, using 250 ml (½ pint) bottled citrus mojo marinade in place of the beer, garlic and lime juice marinade.

### grilled prawn skewers with coriander salsa
Prepare the basic recipe, then serve with coriander salsa (page 26).

### grilled chicken skewers borrachos
Prepare the basic recipe, using boneless, skinless chicken breast cut into 5-cm (2-in) pieces in place of prawns.

variations

# grilled fish tostadas with pineapple–lime salsa

see base recipe page 179

### grilled fish tostadas with papaya–lime salsa
Prepare the basic recipe, using papaya in place of pineapple.

### grilled chicken tostadas with papaya–lime salsa
Prepare the basic recipe, using boneless, skinless chicken breast in place of fish and papaya in place of pineapple.

### pork carnitas tostadas with papaya–lime salsa
Prepare the basic recipe, using pork carnitas (page 143) in place of fish and papaya in place of pineapple.

### crab & black bean tostadas with papaya–lime salsa
Prepare the basic recipe, using a mixture of 200 g (8 oz) rinsed tinned black beans, 150 g (5 oz) cooked crabmeat, ½ teaspoon ground cumin, 120 ml (4 fl. oz) Mexican crèma or sour cream in place of the seasoned fish and papaya in place of pineapple.

variations

# banana leaf-wrapped fish fillets on the grill

see base recipe page 180

### avocado leaf-wrapped fish fillets on the grill
Prepare the basic recipe, using fresh avocado leaves, soaked in hot water
until pliable and then dried, in place of banana leaf.

### cornhusk-wrapped fish fillets on the grill
Prepare the basic recipe, using fresh cornhusks in place of banana leaf.
If using dried cornhusks, soak them in hot water for several hours, then
drain and pat dry.

### baking paper-wrapped fish fillets on the grill
Prepare the basic recipe, using squares of baking paper in place of
banana leaf.

### banana leaf-wrapped pork on the grill
Prepare the basic recipe, using sliced pork loin in place of fish fillets.

variations

# tequila lime-grilled scallops

see base recipe page 182

### tequila lime-grilled prawns
Prepare the basic recipe, using 1 kg (2 lb) peeled and deveined large prawns in place of scallops.

### tequila lime-grilled salmon
Prepare the basic recipe, using 1 kg (2 lb) salmon fillet in place of scallops.

### tequila lime-grilled sea bass
Prepare the basic recipe, using 1 kg (2 lb) sea bass fillet in place of scallops.

### tequila lime-grilled swordfish
Prepare the basic recipe, using 1 kg (2 lb) swordfish steak in place of scallops.

variations

# lobster tacos with yellow tomato salsa

see base recipe page 183

### salmon tacos with yellow & green tomato salsa
Prepare the basic recipe, using 225 g (½ lb) grilled salmon fillet in place
of lobster and adding 80 g (3 oz) tomatillos to the salsa.

### prawn tacos with yellow tomato salsa
Prepare the basic recipe, using 225 g (½ lb) grilled prawns in place of lobster.

### tuna tacos with yellow & green tomato salsa
Prepare the basic recipe, using 225 g (½ lb) grilled tuna steak in place of
lobster and adding 80 g (3 oz) tomatillos to the salsa.

### swordfish tacos with pumpkin seed salsa
Prepare the basic recipe, using 225 g (½ lb) grilled swordfish steaks in place
of lobster and pumpkin seed salsa (page 25) in place of yellow tomato salsa.

variations

# camarones a la diabla

see base recipe page 184

### vieiras a la diabla
Prepare the basic recipe, using sea scallops in place of prawns.

### yellow-fin tuna a la diabla
Prepare the basic recipe, using yellow-fin tuna steak, cut into 5-cm (2-in) pieces, in place of prawns.

### swordfish a la diabla
Prepare the basic recipe, using swordfish steaks, cut into 5-cm (2-in) pieces, in place of prawns.

### chicken a la diabla
Prepare the basic recipe, using 5-cm (2-in) pieces of boneless, skinless chicken breasts in place of prawns.

variations

# red snapper veracruzano

see base recipe page 186

### baja-style red snapper
Prepare the basic recipe, using a Baja-style sauce instead of the Veracruzano sauce. Mix 60 ml (2 fl. oz) olive oil, 80 g (3 oz) chopped spring onions, 10 g (⅓ oz) chopped fresh flat-leaf parsley, 160 g (6 oz) chopped ripe tomato and the juice of 1 lime. Spread it over the fish before baking.

### yucatán-style red snapper
Prepare the recipe, adding ½ teaspoon freshly grated orange zest and 125 ml (4 fl. oz) orange juice to the sauce. Spread it over the fish before baking.

### red snapper escabeche
Prepare the basic recipe. Transfer the fish to a serving platter and leave to come to room temperature. To the sauce in the baking dish, stir in 2 tablespoons white wine vinegar and 2 tablespoons fresh orange juice. Pour the pan juice mixture over the fish and chill. Serve cold.

### grill-baked red snapper
Prepare the basic recipe, but use a grill-proof metal tin instead of a baking dish. Prepare an indirect heat on your barbecue. Place the pan on the indirectly heated side, close the lid and grill-bake for 20–30 minutes or until the fish is just beginning to flake.

# vegetables

Vegetables, fresh and in season, become zesty

accompaniments to Mexican entrees or stand-alone

dishes. Many of these recipes are family favorites,

such as Chillies Rellenos, served at holiday time.

Others take advantage of whatever is in season in

the garden or at the mercado.

# chillies rellenos

see variations page 218

Fresh-roasted Anaheim or poblano chillies are stuffed with cheese and then fried in an egg batter in this classic dish from Puebla, just east of Mexico City.

8 fresh Anaheim or poblano chillies
450 g (1 lb) Monterey Jack cheese, cut to fit
   inside the chillies
100 g (4 oz) plain flour
2 tbsp olive oil
80 g (3 oz) chopped onion

1 clove garlic, minced
1 (400-g/14-oz) can tomato purée
1 tbsp chopped fresh oregano leaves
salt and pepper to taste
vegetable oil for frying
3 large eggs, separated

Place the chillies on a baking sheet under the grill and grill, turning them over once, until the skins are blackened. Place the chillies in a plastic bag, close, and let them steam for 5 minutes. Remove the skins under cold running water. Keeping the stems intact, slit each chilli ¾ down the length of one side. Carefully spoon out the interior ribs and seeds. Stuff each chilli with a piece of cheese and roll in flour. Set aside.

Heat the olive oil in a saucepan over medium-high heat. Sauté the onion and garlic until golden. Stir in the tomato purée and oregano, season to taste and set aside.

Pour the vegetable oil to a depth of 4 cm (1½ in) in a deep and wide frying pan and heat to 220°C (425°F/Gas mark 7). Beat the egg whites until stiff in a large bowl. Beat the yolks until blended, then fold the whites and yolks together. Working in batches, dip each stuffed chilli in the egg batter, then fry in the hot oil for 2–3 minutes or until lightly browned. Remove from the heat, and drain on kitchen towels. Serve topped with the tomato sauce.

*Serves 4–6*

# black bean & roasted tomato tamales

see variations page 219

This vegetarian version of tamales has wonderful colour and flavour. "Tamal" is the singular of tamales.

480 g (1 lb) coarsely chopped yellow tomatoes
1 tbsp olive oil
1 tbsp fresh lime juice
salt and pepper to taste
1 (400-g/14-oz) can black beans
2 cloves garlic, minced

$^1/_2$ tsp ground cumin
$^1/_2$ tsp dried oregano leaves
10 dried cornhusks, soaked in water for
    30 minutes and drained
200 g ($7^1/_2$ oz) corn masa flour
300 ml (10 fl. oz) vegetable stock

Place the chopped tomatoes on a baking sheet and drizzle with olive oil. Roast at 230°C (450°F/Gas mark 8) for 15 minutes or until blistered. Place in a blender or food processor with the lime juice and process until somewhat smooth. Season to taste and set aside.

In a saucepan, bring the black beans, garlic, cumin and oregano to the boil over a medium-high heat. Reduce the heat and simmer until thickened, about 15 minutes.

Arrange the cornhusks on a flat surface. Place the masa flour in a bowl. Stir in the stock to make a soft dough, adding a little more water if necessary. Divide the dough into 10 portions and form each portion into a ball. Place each ball of dough between two unopened plastic sandwich bags, then press to a 12.5- to 15-cm (5- to 6-in) round in a tortilla press.

Place a tablespoon of roasted yellow tomato sauce and a tablespoon of black beans in the middle of each tortilla. Fold in the sides and place in the damp cornhusk. Fold the sides in, then the ends, to enclose the filling. Secure the ends with string so that each tamal is completely enclosed in the husk. Place the tamales vertically in a steamer; do not let them touch the water. Steam for 30 minutes or until the husks pull away from the filling. To serve, unwrap each tamal and serve with more roasted yellow tomato sauce.

*Serves 4–6*

# sizzling mushroom fajitas

see variations page 220

Beef-tasting portabello mushrooms, in place of traditional beef or chicken, make delicious fajitas, too. Serve with store-bought or homemade flour tortillas (page 16), guacamole (page 30) and pico de gallo (page 15).

750 g (1½ lb) portabello mushrooms
1 large onion, sliced into 2.5-cm (1-in) rounds
1 red pepper, stemmed, deseeded and
   cut into quarters
vegetable oil

salt and pepper to taste
flour tortillas, guacamole and pico de gallo
   (store-bought or homemade), for serving

Prepare a hot barbecue or heat a cast-iron fajita pan on the hob until very hot. Brush the mushrooms, onion slices and red pepper with vegetable oil and season to taste. Grill the onion and pepper for 5–7 minutes per side or until charred and softened. Grill the mushrooms for 1½–2 minutes per side or until you have good grill marks. Slice the mushrooms on the diagonal and serve with the grilled vegetables, tortillas, guacamole and pico de gallo.

*Serves 4*

# fresh sweetcorn flan

see variations page 221

The Spanish conquistadors brought their love of flan to Mexico. Today, the most common flans are caramel custard and orange flan, but not all flans are sweet. These individual fresh sweetcorn flans make an easy yet elegant side dish. Pair them with the salsa of your choice as a sauce.

800 g (1 lb 12 oz) fresh or frozen and thawed
   corn kernels
360 ml (12 fl. oz) single cream
6 large eggs

1 tsp salt
1 tsp ground dried ancho or chipotle chilli or
   bottled chipotle sauce
salsa or mole of your choice

Preheat the oven to 175°C (350°F/Gas mark 5). Grease the insides of eight 150-g (6-oz) ramekins and place in a deep baking pan with enough hot water to come halfway up the sides of the ramekins. Place the sweetcorn in a food processor and process until smooth. Add the single cream, eggs, salt and ground ancho, and process until smooth.

Divide the mixture among the prepared ramekins. Bake for 25 minutes or until a knife inserted in the centre of a flan comes out clean. Loosen the flans with a knife and invert onto serving plates. Serve with the salsa or mole of your choice.

*Serves 8*

# three sisters vegetable stew

see variations page 222

The "three sisters" – corn, beans and squash – have been grown by indigenous Mexican peoples for thousands of years. The men slash and burn a plot and the women plant the seeds and tend the garden. The beans use the corn stalks for support. The squash helps repel weeds around both, so the "sisters" work harmoniously together, as in this recipe.

2 tbsp olive oil
1 large onion, chopped
4 garlic cloves, minced
340 g (12 oz) fresh or frozen corn kernels
300 g (10 oz) chopped fresh or frozen butternut
    or acorn squash

1 large dried chipotle chilli
1 l (2 pints) vegetable or chicken stock
1 (400-g/14-oz) can pinto beans, with juice
salt and pepper to taste
chopped fresh flat-leaf parsley and spring onion,
    to garnish

Heat the oil in a large saucepan over medium-high heat. Sauté the onion and garlic until transparent, about 7 minutes. Stir in the corn, squash, chipotle and broth. Bring to the boil, then reduce the heat and simmer for 15 minutes or until the squash and chipotle are tender. Remove the chipotle, chop finely and return to the pan along with the pinto beans. Cook, stirring, until the stew is hot. Season to taste. Serve in bowls garnished with flat-leaf parsley and chopped spring onion.

*Serves 4–6*

# slow-simmered black beans

see variations page 223

A pot of frijoles negras or black beans is often simmering in a Mexican kitchen, as these beans can feature as a side dish at any meal. They're also delicious turned into a salsa, soup or a filling for a taco or burrito. Mexican cooks often add the herb epazote to beans as they're cooking; the herb adds a flavour similar to oregano and also aids in digesting the beans.

60 ml (2 fl. oz) vegetable oil
1 large onion, chopped
2 cloves garlic, chopped
450 g (1 lb) dried black beans, picked over

1 tsp dried epazote or oregano leaves, crumbled
8 cups water
salt

In a large pot over a medium-high heat, heat the oil, add the onion and garlic and sauté until the onion has softened, about 4 minutes. Stir in the beans, oregano and water, and bring to the boil. Reduce the heat and simmer, covered, until the beans are tender, about 2½ hours. If the beans are too soupy, continue to cook uncovered until thickened. Season to taste.

*Serves 6–8*

# frijoles refritos

see variations page 224

Although often seen on Mexican menus as "refried beans", these pinto beans are actually not fried but cooked in good-quality lard for an authentic flavour and texture. They're also popular as a side dish with any meal.

450 g (1 lb) dried pinto beans, picked over
80 g (3 oz) chopped onion

115 g (4 oz) lard or bacon drippings
salt

Place the beans in a large saucepan with enough cold water to cover them. Leave to stand at room temperature overnight. Drain, then place the beans back in the saucepan. Add the onion and enough water to just cover the beans. Bring to the boil, reduce the heat and simmer, covered, until the beans are tender and will mash easily, about 2½ hours. Remove from the heat and drain, reserving about 250 ml (½ pint) of the cooking liquid. With a potato masher, mash the beans in the pot until they are a blend of smooth and chunky. Add some of the cooking liquid if necessary. Stir in the lard and cook over a medium-high heat, stirring constantly, until the fat has been absorbed and the beans are hot. Season to taste before serving.

*Serves 6–8*

# mexican confetti rice

see variations page 225

Also called arroz a la Mexicana or Spanish rice, this dish rounds out any casual meal.

4 tbsp vegetable oil
1 large onion, chopped
2 cloves garlic, minced
420 g (15 oz) uncooked long-grain rice
1 (400-g/14-oz) tin peeled and chopped
   tomatoes, with liquid

1 (100-g/4-oz) tin green chillies
500 ml (1 pint) chicken stock
10 g (¹/₃ oz) chopped firmly packed
   coriander leaves

Heat the oil in a large saucepan over a medium-high heat. Sauté the onion and garlic until softened, about 4 minutes. Stir in the rice until it is well coated by the onion/garlic mixture. Stir in the tomatoes, chillies and chicken stock, and bring to the boil. Reduce the heat and simmer, covered, for about 25 minutes, adding a little water if necessary, until the rice is tender and the liquid is absorbed. Remove from the heat, stir in the coriander and serve.

*Serves 6–8*

# stuffed poblano chillies with walnut sauce

see variations page 226

Known as chiles en nogada, this classic dish is usually served to celebrate Mexican Independence Day as it has the colours of the Mexican flag – red, green and white.

115 g (4 oz) walnut pieces
130 g (4½ oz) sliced almonds
100 g (4 oz) cream cheese
240 ml (8 fl. oz) single cream
1 tsp sugar
120 ml (4 fl. oz) sour cream or crèma

60 ml (2 fl. oz) dry sherry
¼ tsp ground cinnamon
4 fresh poblano chillies
1 recipe empanada filling (page 42)
fresh parsley and pomegranate seeds, to garnish

First, make the walnut sauce. Place the walnut pieces in a bowl with water to cover and soak for 4 hours at room temperature. Drain the walnuts and place in a food processor with the almonds. Process until finely ground. Transfer the ground nuts to a saucepan over a medium heat and stir in the cream cheese, single cream and sugar. Stir until the cream cheese has melted and the mixture is well blended. Remove from the heat and stir in the sour cream, sherry and cinnamon. Set aside. Place the poblanos on a baking sheet under the grill, and grill, turning the chillies once, until the skins are blackened. Place the poblanos in a plastic bag, close, and leave for 5 minutes. Remove the skins under cold, running water. Keeping the stems intact, slit each chilli ¾ down the length of one side. Carefully spoon out the interior ribs and seeds. Stuff each chilli with the empanada filling. Serve each stuffed chilli accompanied by the walnut sauce. Sprinkle with parsley and pomegranate seeds.

*Serves 4*

# charcoal-grilled sweetcorn with chilli–lime butter

see variations page 227

One of Mexico's great culinary gifts to the world is fresh sweetcorn. When it's at its peak in summer, try it the way mercado vendors like to serve it.

8 ears fresh sweetcorn in the husk
115 g (4 oz) unsalted butter, softened
1 tbsp ground dried chipotle chilli

1 tsp freshly grated lime zest
salt

Pull back the husks from each ear of sweetcorn and remove the corn silk. Pull the husks back over the corn and place in a large bowl of cold water. Soak for 30 minutes.

Mash the butter with the chipotle and lime zest until well blended.

Prepare a hot barbecue or grill. Remove the corn from the water and drain. Slightly open the husks and brush some of the chilli–lime butter on the corn kernels. Close the husk and tie the ends with strips of cornhusk or kitchen twine. Place the ears of corn directly over the fire and grill for 6–8 minutes, turning with tongs as the husks begin to brown. To serve, untie the ears, pull back the husks and brush the kernels with more chilli–lime butter.

*Serves 4-6*

# cinco de mayo grilled vegetable platter with salsa verde

see variations page 228

Cinco de Mayo, Spanish for the "5th of May", is a Mexican national holiday celebrating the victory over the French at Puebla de Los Angeles in 1862. Foods in the colours of the Mexican flag – red, green and white – are popular.

for the salsa verde
1 (380-g/13-oz) can tomatillos, with liquid
1 large onion, peeled and quartered
1 clove garlic
1 (100-g/4-oz) can green chillies
for the vegetables
2 large onions, peeled and sliced
    1 cm (½ in) thick

2 bunches spring onions, trimmed
4 large tomatoes, stemmed, cored and cut into
    2.5-cm- (1-in)-thick slices
olive oil for brushing
salt and pepper
fresh coriander, to garnish

To make the salsa verde, place the tomatillos, onion, garlic and green chillies in a blender or food processor. Process until smooth and set aside.

Prepare a hot barbecue or grill. Brush the vegetables with olive oil and season to taste with salt and pepper. Grill, turning, until you have good grill marks. Arrange the vegetables on a serving platter. Drizzle with salsa verde, garnish with coriander and serve.

*Serves 8*

# grilled poblano & onion strips

see variations page 229

Known as rajas or rags, these strips make a delicious accompaniment to beef dishes of all kinds, as well as a filling for sandwiches, burritos, tacos, enchiladas or quesadillas.

4 fresh poblano chillies
olive oil for brushing
2 large onions, peeled and cut into
    1.2-cm ($1/_2$-in) slices
salt and pepper to taste

Prepare a hot barbecue or grill.

Brush the poblanos with olive oil and grill, turning often, until the skins blister and burn. Transfer to a sealable plastic bag and let them steam and soften. Brush the onions with olive oil and grill until you have good grill marks on both sides, about 10 minutes total. Remove the stems, skin and seeds from the poblanos, then slice into thin strips. Cut the onion slices in half and break apart with a fork into strands. Combine the poblanos and onions and season to taste. Keep the rajas warm until serving.

*Serves 4–6*

variations

# chillies rellenos

see base recipe page 199

### chillies rellenos picadillo
Prepare the basic recipe, using empanada filling (page 42) in place of cheese.

### barbecue-roasted chillies rellenos
Prepare the basic recipe, using the barbecue, instead of the grill,
to roast the chillies before proceeding with the recipe.

### stuffed jalapeños
Prepare the basic recipe, using 24 fresh jalapeños in place of poblanos.

### chillies rellenos en nogada
Prepare the basic recipe without the tomato sauce. Top the filled chillies with
the walnut sauce.

variations

# black bean & roasted tomato tamales

see base recipe page 200

### wild mushroom tamales
Prepare the basic recipe, using 300 g (10 oz) sautéed wild mushrooms in place of black beans.

### vegetable tamales
Prepare the basic recipe, using 300 g (10 oz) sautéed vegetables in place of black beans.

### smoky cheese & herb tamales
Prepare the basic recipe, using 260 g (15 oz) grated smoked mozzarella mixed with 10 g (⅓ oz) fresh chopped coriander in place of black beans.

### picadillo tamales
Prepare the basic recipe, using 400 g (1 lb) empanada filling (page 42) in place of black beans.

# sizzling mushroom fajitas

see base recipe page 202

### sizzling vegetable fajitas

Prepare the basic recipe, using strips of fresh courgette, cut 1 cm (½ in) thick, in place of mushrooms.

### sizzling sweetcorn fajitas

Prepare the basic recipe, using 4 ears of fresh sweetcorn, grilled on all sides, in place of mushrooms. With a paring knife, remove the grilled corn kernels and mix with the grilled vegetables.

### sizzling black bean fajitas

Prepare the basic recipe, using 400 g (1 lb) warm tinned black beans in place of grilled mushrooms.

### sizzling salmon fajitas

Grill a 450-g (1-lb) skinless salmon fillet, brushed on both sides with olive oil, over a high heat for 4 minutes per side as you're grilling the vegetables. Cut the salmon into pieces and serve in the tortillas. Top with grilled vegetables and a dollop of authentic guacamole (page 30).

# fresh sweetcorn flan

see base recipe page 205

### fresh squash flan
Prepare the basic recipe, using cooked butternut or acorn squash in place of sweetcorn.

### fresh pumpkin flan
Prepare the basic recipe, using cooked pumpkin in place of sweetcorn.

### fresh hominy flan
Prepare the basic recipe, using tinned, drained hominy in place of sweetcorn.

### roasted vegetable & goat's cheese flan
Prepare the basic recipe, using 450 (15 oz) roasted vegetables and 130 g (4½ oz) fresh goat's cheese in place of sweetcorn.

### fresh courgette flan
Prepare the basic recipe, replacing the sweetcorn with cooked courgette.

# three sisters vegetable stew

see base recipe page 206

### three sisters vegetable & chorizo stew
Prepare the basic recipe, adding 450 g (1 lb) cooked and chopped chorizo to the stew with the pinto beans.

### three sisters vegetable & pork stew
Prepare the basic recipe, adding 300 g (10 oz) pork carnitas (page 143) to the stew with the pinto beans.

### three sisters grilled-vegetable stew
Grill a bunch of spring onions and 2 medium courgettes, then chop. Prepare the basic recipe, adding the onion and courgette in place of the squash.

### three sisters summer vegetable stew
Prepare the basic recipe, adding 150 g (5 oz) chopped courgette and 150 g (5 oz) chopped yellow squash in place of butternut, then proceed with the recipe.

variations

# slow-simmered black beans

see base recipe page 208

### slow-simmered teppary beans
Prepare the basic recipe, using dried teppary beans (or any dried, heirloom bean) in place of black beans.

### slow-simmered chipotle black beans
Prepare the basic recipe, adding 2 tinned chipotle chillies in adobo sauce, chopped, to the onion and garlic.

### pantry shelf black beans
Heat 2 (400-g/14-oz) cans black beans, drained, in a saucepan with 80 g (3 oz) finely chopped onion, 80 g (3 oz) finely chopped boiled ham, 1 teaspoon chopped garlic, and 1 teaspoon dried oregano. Bring to a simmer and cook for 15 minutes to let the flavours blend. Season to taste with salt and pepper.

### moors & christians
Prepare the basic recipe, serving the black beans over coconut rice (page 225).

# frijoles refritos

see base recipe page 209

### vegetarian frijoles refritos
Prepare the basic recipe, using 120 ml (4 fl. oz) vegetable oil in place of lard.

### pantry shelf frijoles refritos
Heat 2 (400-g/14-oz) cans pinto beans, drained, in a saucepan with 80 g
(3 oz) finely chopped onion and 115 g (4 oz) lard. Bring to a simmer and cook
for 15 minutes to let the flavours blend. Season to taste with salt and pepper.

### black beans refritos
Prepare the basic recipe, replacing half the quantity of pinto beans with
black beans.

# mexican confetti rice

see base recipe page 210

### vegetarian confetti rice
Prepare the basic recipe, using vegetable stock in place of chicken stock and proceed with the recipe.

### confetti rice ole!
Prepare the basic recipe, using 1 stemmed, deseeded and chopped small jalapeño in place of tinned, and adding 40 g (1½ oz) chopped fresh yellow pepper and 40 g (1½ oz) chopped fresh orange pepper.

### ancho confetti rice
Prepare the basic recipe, adding 1 teaspoon dried ground ancho chilli to the chicken stock.

### coconut rice
Prepare the basic recipe, using 40 g (2 oz) flaked fresh or dried coconut (not sweetened flaked coconut) in place of the tomatoes and 120 ml (4 fl. oz) cream of coconut in place of the chillies. (This is traditionally served with slow-simmered black beans or fish dishes.)

variations

# stuffed poblano chillies with walnut sauce

see base recipe page 212

### stuffed poblano chillies with pumpkin seed salsa
Prepare the basic recipe, using pumpkin seed salsa (page 25) in place of walnut sauce.

### stuffed poblano chillies with yellow tomato salsa
Prepare the basic recipe, using yellow tomato salsa (page 183) in place of walnut sauce.

### stuffed poblano chillies with salsa cruda
Prepare the basic recipe, using salsa cruda (page 21) in place of walnut sauce.

### fried stuffed poblano chillies
Prepare the basic recipe without the walnut sauce. Separate 3 large eggs. Pour vegetable oil to a depth of 4 cm (1½ in) in a deep and wide frying pan and heat to 220°C (425°F/Gas mark 7). Beat the egg whites until stiff in a large bowl. Beat the yolks until blended, then fold the whites and yolks together. Dip each stuffed chilli in the egg batter and fry in hot oil for 2–3 minutes or until lightly browned.

variations

# charcoal-grilled corn with chilli–lime butter

see base recipe page 213

### charcoal-grilled chillies with chilli–lime butter
Prepare the basic recipe, using 4 Anaheim and 4 poblano chillies in place of
sweetcorn. Grill the peppers whole, turning often, until blistered on all sides.
Stem, seed and slice. Serve with the butter.

### charcoal-grilled potatoes with chilli–lime butter
Prepare the basic recipe, using 4 baking potatoes in place of sweetcorn. Prick
the potatoes all over and par-cook in the microwave for 5 minutes. Cut
lengthways into 1-cm (½-in) slices and brush with some of the butter. Grill
for 2–3 minutes per side or until done. Serve with the remaining butter.

### charcoal-grilled mixed vegetables with chilli–lime butter
Prepare the basic recipe, using 2 medium yellow squash and 2 medium
courgettes in place of sweetcorn. Trim the ends of the squash, slice in half
lengthways and brush with some of the butter. Grill for 2–3 minutes per side
or until you have good grill marks. Serve with the remaining butter.

variations

# cinco de mayo grilled vegetable platter with salsa verde

see base recipe page 214

### cinco de mayo grilled vegetable platter with chilli–lime butter
Prepare the basic recipe, using melted chilli–lime butter (page 213) in place of salsa verde.

### cinco de mayo grilled vegetable platter with chipotle–lime vinaigrette
Prepare the basic recipe, using chipotle–lime vinaigrette (page 69) drizzled over the salad in place of salsa verde.

### cinco de mayo roasted vegetable platter with salsa verde
Prepare the basic recipe, placing the vegetables on a baking sheet in a 230°C (450°F/Gas mark 8) oven until browned and blistered, about 20 minutes.

### cinco de mayo grilled vegetable platter with pumpkin seed salsa
Prepare the basic recipe, using pumpkin seed salsa (page 25) in place of salsa verde.

variations

# grilled poblano & onion strips

see base recipe page 217

### grilled whole poblanos & salad onions
Prepare the basic recipe, using large salad onions in place of white onions.
Grill the salad onions whole, then slice into strips.

### roasted poblano & onion strips
Prepare the basic recipe, placing the vegetables on a baking sheet in a 230°C
(450°F/Gas mark 8) oven until browned and blistered (about 20 minutes).

### sautéed poblano & onion strips
Prepare the basic recipe, using stemmed, deseeded and sliced poblanos
in place of whole poblanos. Heat the olive oil in a large frying pan over
a medium-high heat and sauté the poblano strips and onion slices until
browned and tender (about 10 minutes).

### grilled pepper & onion strips
Prepare the basic recipe, using whole yellow and red peppers in place of
whole poblanos.

# desserts

In the easy-going Mexican culture, sweet things are for any time of day. Rice or bread pudding for breakfast. Bunuelos with a mug of warm Champurrado on a chilly afternoon. Cakes, flans and ice creams on festive occasions or simply after a family dinner.

# bunuelos

see variations page 245

Flour tortillas, lightly fried in oil, are then dusted with cinnamon sugar for a simple, sweet finish to a meal. Served with warm chocolate champurrado (page 268), bunuelos are also one of the ways families welcome friends and loved ones during the holidays. For the best flavour, grind your own cinnamon in a clean coffee or spice grinder.

200 g (8 oz) sugar
4 (7.5-cm/3-in) sticks cinnamon, ground in a
    coffee or spice grinder (or 30 g/1 oz
    ground cinnamon)

1 recipe homemade flour tortillas (page 16) or
    12 shop-bought flour tortillas
vegetable oil for frying

Mix the sugar and ground cinnamon together in a bowl. Set aside.

Pour the vegetable oil into a deep frying pan to a depth of 2.5 cm (1 in). Heat the oil to 190°C (375°F/Gas mark 5). Fry the tortillas, 1 or 2 at a time, until golden brown and crisp, about 30–60 seconds per side. Remove with tongs, drain on kitchen towels and sprinkle liberally on both sides with cinnamon sugar.

*Makes 1 dozen*

# mexican wedding cookies

see variations page 246

Dusted with icing sugar, these festive cookies are tender, buttery and delicious. Grind the almonds in a food processor or a nut grinder before using.

675 g (1 lb 7 oz) unsalted butter, softened
2 tbsp icing sugar
1 large egg yolk
1 tsp vanilla extract

40 g (2 oz) ground almonds
350 g (12 oz) plain flour
260 g (9 oz) icing sugar for dusting

Preheat the oven to 135°C (275°F). Line 2 baking sheets with baking paper and set aside. In a mixing bowl, cream the butter and 2 tbsp icing sugar together with an electric mixer until light and fluffy. Beat in the egg yolk, vanilla and almonds. Beat in the flour, a little at a time, until well blended. Pinch off tablespoon-size pieces of dough and roll into a ball. Place balls 5 cm (2 in) apart on the prepared baking sheets. Bake for 45 minutes or until lightly browned. Leave to cool on the baking sheets until slightly warm.

Sift the remaining icing sugar onto a sheet of baking paper. Gently roll each cookie in the sugar until well coated. Store in airtight containers for up to 3 days.

*Makes 3 dozen cookies*

# mango ice cream

see variations page 247

This fresh-tasting, easy-to-make frozen treat is just what you want on a hot day or after a spicy meal.

2 large, ripe mangoes, peeled, deseeded
    and chopped
65g (2$^1/_2$ oz) sugar
240 ml ( 8 fl. oz) double cream
1 tbsp fresh lemon or lime juice

Place the mangoes, sugar, cream and lemon juice in a food processor and process until smooth. Pour the mixture into an ice cream maker and freeze according to the manufacturer's directions.

*Makes 1 l (2 pints)*

# mexican rice pudding

see variations page 248

The Spanish conquistadors brought their love of rice dishes to Mexico in the 1500s. This comfort food classic, known as arroz con leche, is wonderful at any meal.

2 l (4 pints) whole milk
200 g (8 oz) sugar
$^1/_4$ tsp salt
2 cinnamon sticks, plus 8 more for garnish
420 g (15 oz) short-grain rice, rinsed

1 (400-g/14-oz) tin sweetened condensed milk
1 tbsp vanilla extract
1 cup dried fruit, such as sultanas or dried
  mango, soaked in warm water to soften
1 100 g (4 oz) Mexican chocolate for grating

Place the milk, sugar, salt and cinnamon sticks in a large saucepan, and bring to the boil over a medium-high heat. Stir in the rice, reduce the heat and simmer, covered, until tender, about 15 minutes. Remove from the heat and stir in the sweetened condensed milk and vanilla. Drain the dried fruit and stir it into the rice pudding.

Serve the pudding warm or chilled, garnished with a cinnamon stick and a dusting of grated Mexican chocolate.

*Serves 8*

# passion fruit sorbet

see variations page 249

Many large supermarkets now carry frozen tropical fruit pulp, which makes it easy to get the flavour of Mexico in a frozen treat. Make a simple syrup of water and sugar, then blend in the frozen pulp and flavourings and freeze in an ice cream maker. Passion fruit, known as parcha in Mexico, are small, seedy fruits with a sweet-tart flavour.

250 ml (½ pint) water
200 g (8 oz) sugar
1 (400-g/14-oz) packet passion fruit pulp,
    slightly thawed (or use freshly puréed
    passion fruit)

1/4 tsp freshly grated lime zest
2 tbsp fresh lime juice
mint sprigs, to garnish (optional)

In a saucepan, bring the water and sugar to the boil, stirring until the sugar dissolves. Remove from the heat and leave to cool. Stir the passion fruit pulp, lime zest and juice into the syrup. Pour the mixture into an ice cream maker and freeze according to the manufacturer's directions.

*Makes about 500 ml (1 pint)*

# hacienda-style flan

see variations page 250

Large-acre estates known as haciendas usually concentrate on one regional agricultural product: agave for mescal and tequila in Zacatecas, sugar in Morelos, coffee in Oaxaca, sisal in Yucatán and cattle in Querétaro. During the centuries of Spanish and French colonial rule, haciendas were the power bases of the gentry, with each known for the quality of its kitchen.

300 g (10 oz) fresh pineapple chunks
   (2.5 cm/1-in)
375 ml (12 fl. oz) whole milk
1 vanilla pod, split lengthways
125 ml (4 fl. oz) tequila or rum

3 large eggs
3 large egg yolks
160 g (6 oz) sugar
2 tbsp plain flour
2 tbsp double cream

Preheat the oven to 200°C (400°F/Gas mark 6). Butter a 25-cm (10-in) shallow baking or soufflé dish. Scatter the pineapple chunks over the bottom. Bake until the pineapple caramelizes, about 20 minutes. Remove from the oven and reduce the temperature to 175°C (350°F/Gas mark 5).

Heat the milk in a medium saucepan over medium heat. Scrape the vanilla seeds into the milk, then add the vanilla bean. Bring to a simmer. Remove from the heat and let steep 15 minutes. Remove the vanilla pod and whisk in the tequila or rum. In a medium bowl, whisk the eggs, egg yolks, sugar, flour and cream until smooth. Gradually whisk in the hot milk. Pour the mixture over the pineapple. Bake until a knife inserted in the centre comes out clean, about 30 minutes. Serve warm or at room temperature, spooned into bowls.

*Serves 8*

# mexican chocolate ice cream

see variations page 251

Made with sugar, almonds and cinnamon, each small disc of Mexican chocolate has most of the flavourings you need to make this ice cream.

8 large egg yolks
200 g (8 oz) sugar
500 ml (1 pint) milk, heated until hot
450 g (1 lb) Mexican chocolate, grated

1 tsp vanilla extract
grated chocolate and toasted sliced almonds,
    to garnish

In a large saucepan, whisk the egg yolks and sugar together until light yellow, about 3–5 minutes. Slowly whisk in half of the hot milk until well blended. Place the saucepan over a medium-high heat and whisk in the remaining hot milk. Cook, whisking occasionally, until the mixture coats the back of a spoon, about 10 minutes. Remove from the heat, add the grated chocolate and vanilla and whisk to blend and melt the chocolate. When the mixture is smooth, leave to cool down to room temperature.

Pour the mixture into an ice cream maker and freeze according to manufacturer's directions. To serve, spoon the ice cream into dishes and garnish with grated chocolate and almonds.

*Serves 8*

# capirotada

see variations page 252

This Mexican bread pudding features the caramel flavour of piloncillo or Mexican brown sugar. Capirotada means "a little bit of everything", from leftover bread to sugar, nuts, spices, fruits and cheese.

200 g (8 oz) crumbled piloncillo or light
    brown sugar
250 ml ($^1/_2$ pint) water
2 cinnamon sticks
1 tbsp freshly grated orange zest

180 g (6 oz) cubed bread, toasted
85 g ($3^1/_2$ oz) toasted pine nuts
85 g ($3^1/_2$ oz) toasted, slivered almonds
75 g (3 oz) raisins or dried mango
225 g (8 oz) Monterey Jack cheese, cubed

Preheat the oven to 175°C (350°F/Gas mark 5). Grease the inside of a 23 x 33-cm (9 x 13-in) baking dish and set aside. In a saucepan, bring the sugar, water and cinnamon to the boil over a medium-high heat. Cook until slightly thickened, about 5 minutes. Remove from the heat and stir the orange zest into the syrup. Arrange the bread cubes in the prepared baking dish and top them with the pine nuts, almonds, raisins and cheese. Pour the syrup over the bread cubes and toss with a fork to blend. Bake, covered, for 25 minutes. Uncover and bake for 5 minutes more.

*Serves 8–10*

# cajeta chocolate cake

see variations page 253

This rich, moist version of tres leches (three milks) cake has a cajeta (caramel) topping.

for the cajeta
1 (350-g/12¹/₂-oz) can
    evaporated goat's milk
200 g (8 oz) sugar
2 tbsp butter
1 tsp vanilla extract
salt to taste

for the cake
1 (500-g/18¹/₄-oz) package
    devil's food cake mix
1 (400-g/14-oz) can sweetened
    condensed milk
1 (375-g/12-oz) can
    evaporated milk

125 ml (4 fl. oz) milk
225 g (8 oz) package cream
    cheese at room temperature
5 large eggs
1 tsp vanilla extract

Stir the milk, sugar and butter together in a large saucepan over high heat. Bring to the boil. Cook, whisking often, for 10 minutes. Continue cooking and whisking constantly until the mixture begins to turn medium-brown, about 10 more minutes. Remove from the heat and stir in the vanilla. The sauce should flow from a spoon and will thicken as it cools. After the Cajeta cools, taste and add a little salt if necessary. Preheat oven to 175°C (350°F/ Gas mark 5). Grease and flour a large Kugelhopf tin. Pour the Cajeta into the prepared tin. Prepare the cake mix according to package directions. Pour the cake batter on top of the Cajeta. In a blender or food processor, combine the three milks with the cream cheese, eggs and vanilla. Pour the mixture into the pan so it covers the top of the cake batter. Cover the Kugelhopf tin with foil and place in a larger baking tin. Add enough hot water to reach 5 cm (2 in) up the sides of the Kugelhopf tin. Bake, covered, for 2 hours or until a cocktail stick inserted near the centre comes out clean. Remove from the oven and leave to cool, then remove the foil. Invert the cake onto a large plate or serving dish so the Cajeta drips down the sides of the cake. Refrigerate for at least 1 hour before serving.

*Serves 12–16*

# bunuelos

see base recipe page 231

### sweet orange bunuelos
Replace the cinnamon with 2 tablespoons orange zest.

### chilli–spice bunuelos
Prepare the basic recipe, adding 1 teaspoon ground chipotle or ancho chilli to
the cinnamon sugar.

### sweet bunuelos chips
On a flat surface, stack 4 tortillas on top of each other, making 3 stacks of
tortillas. Using a pizza wheel or a sharp knife, slice each tortilla stack into
8 triangles. Fry the triangles in batches until golden brown and crisp, about
30–60 seconds. Remove with a slotted spoon, drain on kitchen towels and
sprinkle with cinnamon sugar.

### torta de bunuelos
Prepare the basic recipe. In a blender or food processor, process 260 g
(9 oz) queso fresco or curd cheese with 500 ml (1 pint) double cream and
1 teaspoon vanilla extract until somewhat smooth. Thinly spread 1 prepared
bunuelo with 3 tablespoons of this mixture, then stack another bunuelo on
top. Repeat the process until all the filling is used and you have a big stack of
bunuelos. Let rest to slightly soften, then cut into wedges to serve.

# mexican wedding cookies

see base recipe page 232

### walnut wedding cookies
Prepare the basic recipe, using walnuts in place of almonds.

### pecan wedding cookies
Prepare the basic recipe, using pecans in place of almonds.

### mexican wedding sandwich cookies
Prepare the basic recipe. Spread a teaspoon of prepared cajeta (page 244) or dulce de leche on the bottom of one cookie, then place the bottom of a second cookie on the filling to sandwich the two together.

### lemon–almond wedding cookies
Prepare the basic recipe, adding 1 teaspoon lemon zest to the cookie dough before forming balls.

# mango ice cream

see base recipe page 234

### papaya ice cream
Prepare the basic recipe, using 600 g (1 lb 4 oz) fresh, ripe papayas in place
of mangoes.

### guava ice cream
Prepare the basic recipe, using 600 g (1 lb 4 oz) fresh and ripe or tinned
guavas in place of mangoes.

### banana ice cream
Prepare the basic recipe, using 600 g (1 lb 4 oz) fresh, ripe bananas in place
of mangoes.

### a trio of mexican ice creams
Prepare three of the ice creams and serve a scoop of each on each
dessert plate.

### avocado ice cream
Prepare the basic recipe, using 3 ripe avocados, pitted and chopped, in place
of the mangoes.

variations

# mexican rice pudding

see base recipe page 237

### mexican rice pudding with fresh berries
Prepare the basic recipe, using 150 g (5 oz) fresh berries (not soaked in water) in place of the dried fruit.

### mexican rice pudding with roasted pineapple
Prepare the basic recipe, using roasted pineapple chunks in place of the dried fruit. To prepare the pineapple, toss 150 g (5 oz) fresh pineapple chunks with 1 tablespoon brown sugar and roast at 230°C (450°F/Gas mark 8) for 15 minutes.

### mexican rice pudding with mexican chocolate sauce
Prepare the basic recipe. To make the sauce, combine a 100-g (4-oz) disc of Mexican chocolate with 120 ml (4 fl. oz) double cream in a medium saucepan over low heat, stirring until the chocolate melts. Spoon the sauce over each serving of rice pudding.

### breakfast rice pudding
Prepare the basic recipe. Chill the pudding overnight. In the morning, place a spoonful in a bowl and top with fresh berries, toasted nuts and a dollop of crèma.

# passion fruit sorbet

see base recipe page 239

### coconut sorbet
Prepare the basic recipe, using frozen coconut pulp (or freshly grated coconut) in place of passion fruit.

### tropical fruit sorbetti
Prepare both passion fruit and coconut sorbets and serve together in a glass dish, garnished with mint leaves.

### papaya sorbet
Prepare the basic recipe, using frozen papaya pulp (or freshly puréed papaya) in place of passion fruit.

### guava & crème fraîche sorbet
Prepare the basic recipe, using frozen guava pulp (or freshly puréed guava) in place of passion fruit and adding 240 ml (8 fl. oz) crème fraîche.

### tequila and passion fruit slush
Prepare the basic recipe. When frozen, add 60 ml (2 fl. oz) tequila to 1 scoop passion fruit sorbet and blend. Serve immediately in a tall glass.

variations

# hacienda–style flan

see base recipe page 240

### hacienda-style pumpkin flan
Prepare the basic recipe, using fresh pumpkin cubes in place of pineapple.

### hacienda-style squash flan
Prepare the basic recipe, using cubes of fresh butternut squash in place
of pineapple.

### hacienda-style coconut flan
Prepare the basic recipe, using 150 g (5 oz) grated fresh coconut in
place of pineapple. Bake the coconut until it is lightly browned, about
10–15 minutes, then proceed with the recipe.

### hacienda-style papaya flan
Prepare the basic recipe, using cubes of fresh, ripe papaya in place
of pineapple.

variations

# mexican chocolate ice cream

see base recipe page 241

### mexican chipotle–chocolate ice cream
Prepare the basic recipe, adding 1 teaspoon ground dried chipotle with the vanilla.

### mexican chocolate–almond ice cream
Prepare the basic recipe, adding 85 g (3½ oz) toasted, sliced almonds with the vanilla.

### easy mexican chocolate chip ice cream
Grate 200 g (8 oz) Mexican chocolate. Soften 1 l (2 pints) vanilla ice cream. In a bowl, blend the chocolate with the softened ice cream. Cover and freeze.

### mexican coffee & chocolate ice cream
Prepare the basic recipe, adding 25 g (1 oz) ground Mexican coffee to the milk before heating it. Set the coffee-flavoured milk aside to steep for 15 minutes. Line a sieve with muslin and strain the milk into a bowl. Discard the coffee grounds, and proceed with the recipe.

variations

# capirotada

see base recipe page 242

### capirotada with cajeta
Prepare the basic recipe. Warm 1 recipe cajeta (page 244) in a medium saucepan over low heat, stirring until melted. Spoon the sauce over each serving of bread pudding.

### capirotada with blueberries
Prepare the basic recipe, using 150 g (5 oz) fresh blueberries in place of raisins.

### capirotada with sweet mango cream
Prepare the basic recipe. Drizzle each serving with sweet mango cream (page 27).

### capirotada french toast
Prepare the basic recipe, dividing the mixture between 2 (12.5 x 23-cm/ 5 x 9-inch) loaf tins. Bake and allow to cool. Whisk 5 large eggs with 1 tablespoon vanilla extract in a shallow bowl. Slice each loaf of capirotada into 8 slices. Melt 4 tablespoons butter in a large frying pan over a medium-high heat. Dip both sides of each slice into the egg mixture, then shallow-fry until golden on each side, about 4 minutes. To serve, dust each slice with icing sugar.

# cajeta chocolate cake

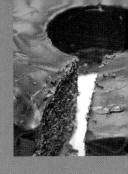

see base recipe page 244

### cajeta spice cake
Prepare the basic recipe, using spice cake mix in place of devil's food.

### pantry cajeta cake
Prepare the basic recipe, using dulce de leche in place of homemade cajeta.

### mexican chocolate cake
Prepare the basic recipe, omitting the cajeta. After baking, cooling and
inverting the cake onto a platter, drizzle warm Mexican chocolate sauce
(page 248) over the cake.

### cajeta orange cake
Prepare the basic recipe, using fairy cake mix in place of devil's food.
Add 1 tablespoon freshly grated orange zest to the cake batter.

# drinks

What would drinks be today without Mexico's contributions of chocolate, vanilla, tequila and coffee? From cocktails to hot chocolate, Mexican ingredients put the "ole" at the beginning and end of a meal.

# world's best margarita

see variations page 271

Made from the blue agave plant that is native to the desert region of western Mexico, tequila evolved from a fermented beverage drunk by the Aztecs. When the Spanish conquistadors ran out of brandy after they landed in 1521, they created tequila, the first distilled beverage in the New World. In Mexico, a margarita is made with native Key limes, the smaller, thinner-skinned version of the more common Persian lime. Use the best-quality tequila for the best flavour.

250 ml ($^1/_2$ pint) fresh lime juice
250 ml ($^1/_2$ pint) Grand Marnier or Triple Sec
500 ml (1 pint) tequila
wedges of fresh lime
salt, optional

Pour the lime juice, Grand Marnier and tequila in a large jug, and stir. Use a wedge of lime to wipe the rim of each margarita glass, then dip each rim into a saucer of salt, if you like.

Choose one of several ways of serving: Stir the margarita mixture with crushed ice, then strain into a glass for a straight margarita. Pour the mixture into a glass full of crushed ice for a margarita on the rocks. Or freeze the margarita mixture for at least 8 hours or until just slushy, then pour or spoon into glasses.

*Serves 20*

# mexican mojito

see variations page 272

While the original Cuban mojito is based on rum, the Mexican mojito uses tequila and Key limes for more flavour.

10 fresh mint leaves, plus 1 sprig for garnish
juice of 2 Persian or 4 Key limes
85 ml (3$\frac{1}{2}$ fl. oz) water
2 tbsp caster sugar
1 cup crushed ice
40 ml (1$\frac{1}{2}$ fl. oz) tequila

Tear the mint leaves in half and place them in a cocktail shaker. Using a muddler or the end of a wooden spoon, mash the leaves until bruised and fragrant. Add the lime juice, water, sugar, ice and tequila. Cover the shaker and shake briskly. Pour into a tall glass and garnish with a mint sprig.

*Serves 1*

# michelada

see variations page 273

The Michelada beer cocktail, slang for "my cold beer", originated in northern Mexico in the 1940s as a simple combination of beer, salt, lime and ice. Now, each bar has its own take.

1 wedge fresh lime
coarse salt
1 small bottle Mexican beer, such as Tecate or
    Dos Equis, very cold

60 ml (2 fl. oz) fresh lime juice
1 tsp Worcestershire sauce
1–2 dashes bottled pepper sauce

Use the wedge of lime to wipe the rim of a glass with juice, then dip the rim into a saucer of salt. Fill the glass halfway with ice. Pour in the beer, lime juice, Worcestershire and pepper sauce. Stir with a spoon. Drink, then top up with the rest of the beer as needed.

*Serves 1*

# summer fruit coolers

see variations page 274

Street vendors in Mexican towns often serve a refreshing drink called agua fresca, based on fruit juices and purées as well as the tart hibiscus or Jamaica flower, tropical tamarind and even fresh cucumber. In a rainbow of colours, these drinks are sometimes served from barrel-shaped glass jars called vitroleros.

300 g (10 oz) deseeded, peeled and coarsely
    chopped cantaloupe or honeydew melon
2–4 tbsp sugar
2–4 tbsp fresh lime juice
500 ml (1 pint) water

In a blender, purée the fruit. Season to taste with sugar and lime juice until flavourful and tangy. Stir the fruit mixture and water together in a jug and serve over ice.

*Serves 4*

# sangrita with a tequila chaser

see variations page 275

Served in tall frosty glasses, sangrita – with its accompanying shot of tequila – is a bracing cure for a hangover or a way to wake up a sleepy afternoon. It's like a deconstructed Bloody Mary, only more citrus-flavoured, and with a spring onion as a swizzle stick.

250 ml ($^1/_2$ pint) tomato juice
500 ml (1 pint) fresh orange juice
125 ml (4 fl. oz) fresh lime juice
1/4 tsp bottled pepper sauce
4 spring onions, trimmed slightly on both ends
4 shots tequila in individual shot glasses

Combine the juices and pepper sauce in a large jug. Stir to blend. Pour into frosty glasses over ice. Add a spring onion to each glass. Serve each glass with a shot glass of tequila.

*Serves 4*

# prickly pear lemonade

see variations page 276

Prickly pear is the dark red fruit of a cactus that grows in the deserts of northern and western Mexico. It has a flavour similar to kiwi fruit and is delicious in this rosy-coloured take on lemonade.

1 l (2 pints) water
juice of 6 lemons, plus 1 sliced lemon for
    garnish
120 ml (4 fl. oz) prickly pear juice or syrup (or
    use tinned pear syrup)

130 g (4$^1$/$_2$ oz) sugar

In a large jug, stir the water, lemon juice, prickly pear juice, and sugar together until the sugar dissolves. To serve, pour over ice in a tall glass and garnish with a lemon slice.

*Serves 6*

# sangria

see variations page 277

Brought from Spain to Mexico, refreshing sangria is usually served in earthenware or glass jugs with antojitos or appetizers.

500 ml (1 pint) fresh orange juice
125 ml (4 fl. oz) Grand Marnier or Triple Sec
1 bottle (750 ml) light red or rosé wine
50 g (2 oz) sugar
1 orange, thinly sliced
1 lime, thinly sliced

Combine all ingredients in a large jug and refrigerate until well chilled. Serve over ice, if desired.

*Serves 4–6*

# tequila hot toddy

see variations page 278

Cold weather, runny nose, bad day – these are all good reasons to make a tequila hot toddy for yourself or someone you love.

2 tbsp tequila
2 tbsp honey
1 lemon slice
cinnamon stick (optional)
hot water

Place the tequila, honey, lemon slice and cinnamon stick in a coffee mug. Add hot water and use the cinnamon stick to muddle the lemon and stir the ingredients together. Drink while it's hot.

*Serves 1*

# mexican coffee

see variations page 279

Coffee came to Mexico from the Antilles and has been cultivated in the highlands since the late 18th century. Known as café de olla – after the earthenware pot in which it is traditionally brewed – this coffee also tastes wonderful when made in a percolator. Look for Mexican coffee varieties with "SHG" on the package for "strictly high grown" coffee beans grown in the highest altitude, which contributes to their robust flavour.

45 g (2 oz) ground Mexican coffee
1 (7.5-cm/3-in) cinnamon stick, broken in half
4 tbsp firmly packed dark brown sugar
1 l (2 pints) water

Place the coffee, cinnamon stick pieces and sugar in a coffee filter. Place the water in the percolator. Brew, then pour into cups to serve.

*Serves 4-6*

# champurrado

see variations page 280

A warm, spicy, and milky drink usually served with bunuelos (page 231), champurrado is a favourite during the holiday season. It's thickened with the same masa corn flour used to make corn tortillas.

500 ml (1 pint) warm water
65 g (2¼ oz) corn masa flour
500 ml (1 pint) milk
1 (100-g/4-oz) disc Mexican chocolate,
    finely chopped

4 tbsp firmly packed dark brown sugar
¼ tsp ground aniseed or cinnamon

Combine the water and corn masa in a bowl and whisk until somewhat thickened. Set aside.

Combine the milk, chocolate and sugar in a large saucepan over a medium-high heat and stir until steamy and the chocolate and sugar have melted; do not boil. Whisk in the masa mixture and cook, stirring, for a few minutes more until thickened. Remove from the heat, add the ground aniseed and place the bulbous end of the molinillo in the hot mixture. Place the molinillo handle between your palms and rotate to froth the mixture (or use a wire whisk). Pour into mugs to serve. Strain through a sieve before serving, if you like.

*Serves 4–6*

# mexican hot chocolate

see variations page 281

According to ancient Toltec legend, the god Quetzalcoatl brought seeds of the cacao tree to Earth. These seeds produced one of Mexico's best-known gifts to the food world: chocolate. Mexican chocolate comes as small disks of dark chocolate mixed with cinnamon, sugar and ground almonds. Although this is not quite the dark chocolate beverage that the Aztec ruler Montezuma drank, Mexican hot chocolate is creamy and mildly spicy. To be really authentic, froth it with a molinillo, a turned wood stirrer that you hold between your palms and rotate.

1 l (2 pints) whole milk
1 (100-g/4-oz) disc Mexican chocolate,
    finely chopped

Heat the milk and chocolate in a large saucepan until steamy and the chocolate has melted; do not boil. Remove from the heat and place the bulbous end of the molinillo in the hot chocolate. Place the molinillo handle between your palms and rotate to froth the chocolate (or use a wire whisk). Pour into mugs to serve.

*Serves 4–6*

variations

# world's best margarita

see base recipe page 255

### world's best pomegranate margarita
Prepare the basic recipe, using 125 ml (4 fl. oz) pomegranate juice in place of 125 ml (4 fl. oz) of the lime juice.

### world's best mango margarita
Prepare the basic recipe, using 125 ml (4 fl. oz) mango juice in place of 125 ml (4 fl. oz) of the lime juice.

### world's best passion fruit margarita
Prepare the basic recipe, using 125 ml (4 fl. oz) passion fruit purée in place of 125 ml (4 fl. oz) of the lime juice. To make passion fruit purée, seed and skin a fresh passion fruit, then purée the fruit pulp.

### world's best prickly pear margarita
Prepare the basic recipe, using 125 ml (4 fl. oz) prickly pear purée in place of 125 ml (4 fl. oz) of the lime juice. As a substitute for prickly pear purée, make up the same quantity of puréed canned pears.

variations

# mexican mojito

see base recipe page 256

### mango mojito
Prepare the basic recipe, using mango nectar in place of water.

### lemongrass mojito
Prepare the basic recipe, adding 2 fresh lemongrass stalks about 10 cm (4 in) long. Bruise them along with the mint leaves.

### blackberry mojito
Prepare the basic recipe, using blackberry juice in place of water.

### pineapple mojito
Prepare the basic recipe, using pineapple juice in place of water. Garnish with a spear of fresh pineapple.

variations

# michelada

see base recipe page 257

### macho michelada
Prepare the basic recipe. Serve with a shot of tequila as a chaser.

### tex-mex michelada
Fill a large mug with ice, pour lager over it and squeeze in fresh lime juice to taste.

### mucho gusto michelada
Do not salt the rim. Prepare the basic recipe, using bottled Maggi seasoning in place of Worcestershire sauce and adding ¼ teaspoon celery salt and ¼ teaspoon adobo seasoning to the glass. Adobo seasoning is a mix of garlic powder, onion powder, salt, black pepper, dry oregano and, sometimes, dried citrus zest.

### mexico city michelada
Prepare the basic recipe, adding 250 ml (½ pint) tomato juice to the lime juice.

variations

# summer fruit coolers

see base recipe page 258

### watermelon agua fresca
Prepare the basic recipe, using watermelon in place of the cantaloupe or honeydew.

### mango agua fresca
Prepare the basic recipe, using mango in place of the cantaloupe or honeydew.

### strawberry agua fresca
Prepare the basic recipe, using hulled fresh strawberries in place of the cantaloupe or honeydew.

### tamarind agua fresca
Prepare the basic recipe, using 500 ml (1 pint) tamarind pulp in place of the cantaloupe or honeydew. Strain the tamarind mixture through a sieve before adding to the water.

variations

# sangrita with a tequila chaser

see base recipe page 260

### chipotle sangrita
Prepare the basic recipe, using 125 ml (4 fl. oz) bottled Mexican marinade in place of bottled pepper sauce.

### spicy sangrita
Prepare the basic recipe, using V-8 or a spicy tomato juice in place of plain tomato juice and 125 ml (4 fl. oz) bottled Mexican marinade in place of bottled pepper sauce.

### sangrita cocktail
Prepare the basic recipe, stirring the shot of tequila into the drink before serving.

### virgin sangrita
Prepare the basic recipe, omitting the tequila chaser.

variations

# prickly pear lemonade

*see base recipe page 262*

### prickly pear & mango lemonade
Prepare the basic recipe, adding 250 ml (½ pint) mango nectar.

### lemongrass lemonade
Prepare the basic recipe, omitting the prickly pear juice. Place the water and sugar in a saucepan with 2 (10-cm/4-in) stalks of fresh lemongrass and bring to the boil. Remove from the heat and leave to steep for 30 minutes or until just warm. Stir in the lemon juice and pour over ice in a tall glass.

### mexican hibiscus flower lemonade
Prepare the basic recipe, omitting the prickly pear juice. Place the water and sugar in a saucepan with 3 hibiscus teabags and bring to the boil. Remove from the heat and leave to steep for 30 minutes or until just warm. Stir in the lemon juice and pour over ice in a tall glass.

### hot prickly pear lemonade
Prepare the basic recipe, combining all ingredients in a saucepan over a medium-high heat until hot. Serve in mugs.

variations

# sangria

see base recipe page 263

### white sangria
Prepare the basic recipe, using Chardonnay or another dry white wine in place of red or rosé.

### sangria roja
Prepare the basic recipe, using pomegranate juice in place of orange juice and pomegranate seeds in place of orange slices.

### tropical sangria
Prepare the basic recipe, using Chardonnay or another dry white wine in place of red or rosé wine and mango nectar in place of orange juice.

### sparkling sangria
Prepare the basic recipe, using a cold, sparkling white wine in place of red or rosé. Do not chill, but serve right away over ice.

variations

# tequila hot toddy

see base recipe page 265

### tequila hot toddy with lime
Prepare the basic recipe, using a wedge of fresh lime in place of the lemon slice.

### rum hot toddy
Prepare the basic recipe, using dark rum in place of tequila.

### prickly pear hot toddy
Heat 1 cup of prickly pear lemonade (page 276), add 2 tablespoons tequila and serve hot in a coffee mug.

### really bad day hot toddy
Prepare the basic recipe, using 4 tablespoons tequila.

### virgin toddy
Prepare the basic recipe, using 60 ml (2 fl. oz) cider vinegar in place of the tequila.

# mexican coffee

see base recipe page 266

### spiced mexican coffee
Prepare the basic recipe, adding ½ teaspoon ground cinnamon and ½ teaspoon ground chipotle to the coffee grounds.

### after-dinner mexican coffee
Prepare the basic recipe, adding 1–2 tablespoons of coffee-flavoured liqueur to each cup before pouring in the coffee.

### iced mexican coffee
Prepare the basic recipe, letting the coffee cool. Fill 4 large glasses with ice. Pour 1 tablespoon of single cream in each glass. Pour the coffee into the glasses and stir to blend.

### mexican coffee affogatto
Prepare the basic recipe. To make this sundae, put 2 scoops of vanilla or coffee ice cream in each of 4 bowls. Pour hot coffee over the ice cream and serve.

### mexican coffee with almond liqueur
Prepare the basic recipe, adding a shot of Mexican almond liqueur to each cup just before serving.

variations

# champurrado

see base recipe page 268

### spiced champurrado
Prepare the basic recipe, adding ½ teaspoon ground cinnamon and ½ teaspoon ground dried chipotle in place of the ¼ teaspoon aniseed.

### after-dinner champurrado
Prepare the basic recipe. To serve, add a shot of chocolate liqueur to each mug and top with whipped cream.

### orange champurrado
Prepare the basic recipe, adding 1 tablespoon grated orange zest with the aniseed.

### las posadas champurrado
For the *las posadas* tradition at Christmas serve champurrado in little cups accompanied by a small cookie to friends who stop by.

variations

# mexican hot chocolate

see base recipe page 270

### mexican hot chocolate with tequila
Prepare the basic recipe, adding a shot of tequila to each mug of hot chocolate.

### mexican hot chocolate coffee
Brew 8 cups of coffee. Place 1 tablespoon of crumbled Mexican chocolate in the bottom of each coffee mug and pour in the hot coffee. Stir to blend. Add cream or sugar if desired.

### mexican hot white chocolate drink
Prepare the basic recipe, using 75 g (3 oz) white chocolate chips, 3 tablespoons ground almonds, 1 tablespoon sugar and 2 teaspoons ground cinnamon in place of the Mexican chocolate.

### mexican hot chocolate sundae
Prepare the basic recipe and pour 125 ml (4 fl. oz) hot chocolate over a scoop of vanilla ice cream. Serve immediately.

### hot chocolate with coffee liqueur
Prepare the basic recipe adding a shot of coffee liqueur to each mug of hot chocolate.

# index